Advanced Pattern Block Book

Table of Contents

Introduction

As students progress from the primary grades to middle school, it is important to remember that the use of manipulatives remains a powerful tool in building understanding and applying knowledge. Pattern blocks help students to visualize problems and solutions and provide a high level of engagement. This book is designed to provide teachers with effective ways to use pattern blocks to address the major topics of the math standards:

- Number and Operations
- Measurement
- Geometry
- Algebra
- Statistics and Probability

We have also linked the activities to the NTCM Focal Points and provided a simple form for recording student outcomes.

The first section of the book provides explorations designed to engage students with certain concepts and to get them ready for the topic activities. Most students will be familiar with pattern blocks from earlier grades and will have a positive approach to using them. If possible, have a set of overhead pattern blocks (and projector) on hand to model the activities when appropriate. For a whole class, about 5 complete sets of 250 pattern blocks will be needed. To make them easier to handle, they can be broken into smaller units and stored in plastic bags.

If you have access to a computer and projector or interactive white board, the National Library of Virtual Manipulatives provides an excellent resource for demonstration with pattern blocks. Visit http://nlvm.usu.edu/ and navigate to the appropriate grade level and select the Pattern Blocks applet.

Many activities may generate a range of correct answers; students should be encouraged to predict outcomes and discuss their reasoning. When students have challenges, it is helpful to ask questions that will enable them to learn how to solve problems.

Please share your comments and suggestions with us. We would appreciate hearing from you and your students.

—Vincent Altamuro and Sandra Clarkson

 © Didax – www.didax.com

ADVANCED
PATTERN BLOCK
BOOK

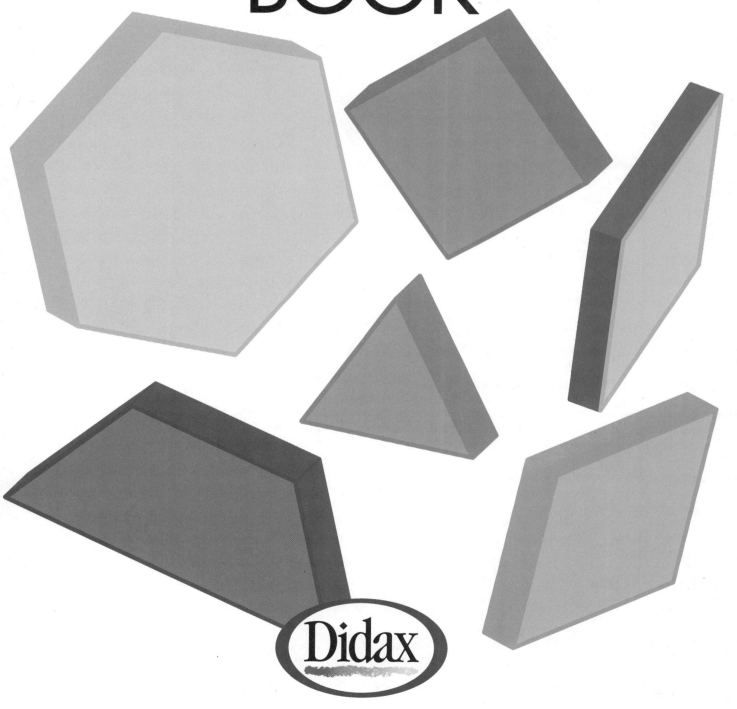

Didax

Vincent Altamuro and Sandra Clarkson

Copyright © 2010 by Didax, Inc., Rowley, MA 01969. All rights reserved.

Limited reproduction permission: The publisher grants permission to individual teachers who have purchased this book to reproduce the blackline masters as needed for use with their own students. Reproduction for an entire school or school district or for commercial use is prohibited.

Printed in the United States of America.

This book is printed on recycled paper.

Order Number 211046
ISBN 978-1-58324-317-6

D E F G H 18 17 16 15 14

395 Main Street
Rowley, MA 01969
www.didax.com

Focal Point Progress Sheet

	Focal Point Outcome	Needs Instruction	Working at Level
Problem Solving	Uses logical thinking to solve problems.		
	Uses guess and check to solve problems.		
	Explains methods and reasoning behind problem-solving strategies.		
	Models problems with physical objects.		
Number & Operations	Recognizes proportional relationships among different pattern blocks.		
	Recognizes that some numbers are divisible only by one and themselves.		
	Understands the concept of equivalency in shapes.		
	Understands the concept of bilateral symmetry.		
	Understands the concept of area equivalence.		
	Understands the concept of one (whole) with fractions.		
	Understands the concept of addition of fractions, with like and unlike denominators.		
	Identifies missing addends.		
Geometry & Measurement	Identifies and names polygons.		
	Classifies polygons by properties of their angles and sides.		
	Applies transformations and symmetry to analyze problem-solving situations.		
	Understands relationships among area and perimeter.		
	Understands the idea of conservation of area—that is, the area of a figure doesn't change even when its parts are rearranged.		
	Identifies obtuse, acute, right, straight, and reflex angles.		
	Determines whether angles are congruent.		
	Understands the concept of degrees in angle measurement.		
Algebra	Uses, represents, and extends patterns.		
	Makes organized lists to solve numerical problems.		
	Writes an equation to represent a function from a table of values.		
	Evaluates formulas for area for given input values.		
	Uses algebraic procedures to solve simple one-step equations.		
	Uses a table to create algebraic patterns and organize data.		
Probability & Statistics	Represents data using bar graphs and uses bar graphs to answer questions.		
	Constructs a frequency table to represent a collection of data.		
	Recognizes that the "value" of a combination of blocks isn't changed when blocks are permuted.		
	Understands the idea of likely outcomes.		
	Understands and applies concepts of probability.		
	Uses fractions/ratios to record experimental results.		

Answer Key

The Answers for all activities in this book are available at www.didax.com/211046.pdf.

© Didax – www.didax.com

Advanced Pattern Block Book

Explore & Discover

Focal Point

Problem Solving – Use logical thinking to solve problems. Use guess and check to solve problems.

Materials

- Quadrilateral pattern blocks
  - squares
  - trapezoids
  - blue & tan rhombuses
- 3 × 3 Force-Out game board (page 3)
- 4 × 4 Force-Out game board (page 134)

Instructions

The object of the game is to place pattern blocks on the 3 × 3 game board so that no color appears twice in the same row, column, or on the principal diagonals of the game board. Players who cannot play a different color on their next move are "forced out."

Have each pair of students select two different quadrilaterals. Each student should use 3 pattern blocks of each kind of quadrilateral (6 blocks per student altogether). Have students decide who will be Player A. Player A begins play by placing his/her block in any square on the game board. Play continues as Players A and B take turns placing blocks in empty squares.

Play continues until a player cannot place a block. Play again with Player B going first. (Note: If there are three players, each player selects a different quadrilateral and uses 4 pattern blocks of that kind of quadrilateral.)

After a player is forced out, the remaining player (or players) is considered the "winner" and given one point. After three games, with players taking turns going first, the player with the most points is the "champion."

Guided Learning

1. If you were Player A, in which square would you put your first block? Why?

2. If you were Player A, in which square would you NOT put your first block?

3. Will there always be a force-out?

4. Is it more helpful to be first in this activity, or does it matter?

5. Name the quadrilaterals used in this activity.

6. How are rhombuses and squares different? The same?

7. How are rhombuses and trapezoids different? The same?

8. Which of the quadrilaterals is not a parallelogram? Explain.

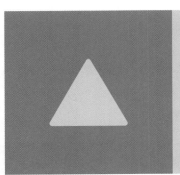

Explore More!

Use the 4 × 4 game board for 4 people (page 134). Each student takes 3 of one kind of pattern block. The students decide who goes first, second, and so on. Follow the instructions above. Is it possible to completely cover a game board using 4 different colors and not have a force-out? See right for the answer!

1	2	3	4
4	3	2	1
2	1	4	3
3	4	1	2

   © Didax – www.didax.com

Name: _____

Directions for 2 Players

1. Decide which two quadrilaterals you want to be and take 3 blocks of each kind, 6 blocks in all. (Example: Player A chooses the blue and tan rhombuses; Player B chooses the trapezoid and square.)

2. Take turns placing a block in any square on the game board. Remember: The same color cannot appear in the same row or column or along the main diagonals.

3. Play continues until a player cannot place a block.

Directions for 3 Players

1. Decide which one quadrilateral you want to be and take 4 blocks of that kind.

2. Follow the directions above.

<table>
<tr><td></td><td></td><td></td></tr>
<tr><td></td><td></td><td></td></tr>
<tr><td></td><td></td><td></td></tr>
</table>

Focal Point

Problem Solving/Geometry – Use physical objects to model the problem. Identify and name polygons. Recognize that each colored pattern block has a geometric name. Recognize the proportional relationships among the different pattern blocks.

Materials

- Pattern blocks:
  - triangles
  - trapezoids
  - blue rhombuses
  - hexagons

Instructions

Have the students do the following:

1. Cover the stars with the indicated number of pattern blocks.

2. See if Star A and Star C can be covered in more than one way.

3. Make a new star (D) using any number of hexagons, trapezoids, blue rhombuses, and/or triangles.

4. Record how many of each block they used in the spaces provided on the worksheet.

Guided Learning

1. Which star used the fewest number of triangles? The most?

2. Why does the number of triangles used vary?

3. What is the relationship between the triangle and the blue rhombus?

4. What is the relationship between the triangle and the trapezoid?

5. What is the relationship between the triangle and the hexagon?

6. What is the geometric name of the blue pattern block? The red pattern block? The yellow pattern block?

Explore More!

Can you make a star with only one color (other than "B")? Can you make a star without using any triangles?

© Didax – www.didax.com

Name: _____

The stars on this page are equal in size. Cover three of the stars with the pattern blocks indicated. Cover the fourth star in any way you want.

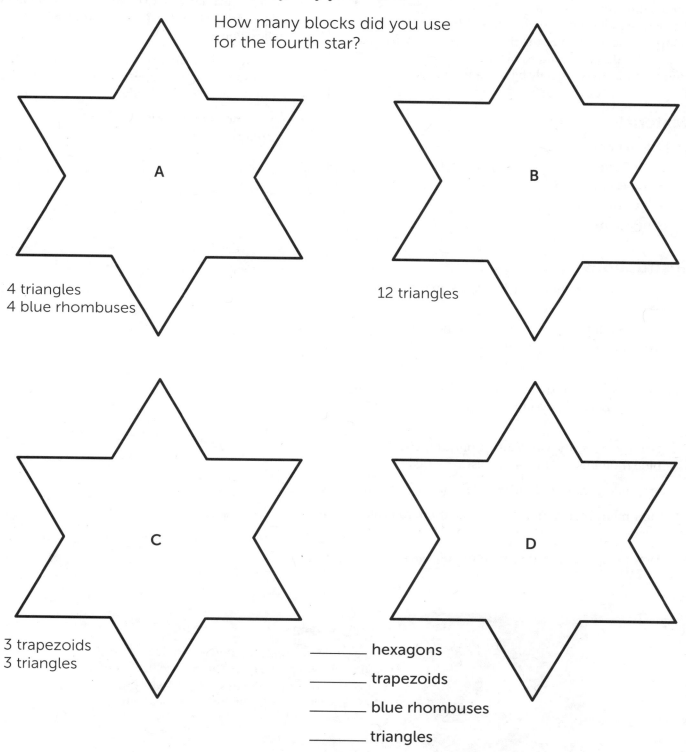

How many blocks did you use for the fourth star?

A

4 triangles
4 blue rhombuses

B

12 triangles

C

3 trapezoids
3 triangles

D

_____ hexagons

_____ trapezoids

_____ blue rhombuses

_____ triangles

© Didax – www.didax.com

Focal Point

Problem Solving/Number – Use physical objects to model the problem. Identify and name polygons. Recognize that each colored pattern block has a geometric name. Recognize the proportional relationships among the different pattern blocks. Recognize that some numbers are divisible only by one and themselves.

Materials

- Pattern blocks:
  - triangles
  - trapezoids
  - blue rhombuses
  - hexagons

Instructions

1. Before the students place hexagons on the Gretle, ask:

   Do you think you can cover the Gretle completely using only hexagons? Why or why not? Prove your answer. Could it be done?

2. Next, have the students make other predictions. Say: You used 2 hexagons but could not cover the Gretle. Ask:

   Can you cover the Gretle using only trapezoids? Only blue rhombuses? Only triangles?

   How many trapezoids do you think you will need?

   How many blue rhombuses do you think you will need?

   How many triangles do you think you will need?

Guided Learning

1. Which blocks will completely cover the Gretle? Why?

2. What is the relationship of hexagons to triangles? Trapezoids to triangles? Blue rhombuses to hexagons?

3. If you need 19 triangles to cover the Gretle, why can't the hexagons or the trapezoids or the rhombuses completely cover the Gretle?

4. What kind of number is 19?
   A prime number

Explore More!

Have the students create a different Gretle that can be covered with trapezoids. Have them trace it. Now can they cover it with only triangles? Why or why not? Now can they cover it with only blue rhombuses? Why or why not?

   © Didax – www.didax.com

Name: _____

This is a Gretle. Cover it with pattern blocks. Remove your blocks.

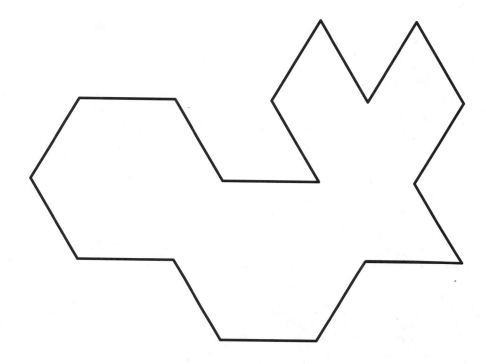

1. Cover the Gretle using only hexagons. Can it be done? _____

2. Cover it using only trapezoids. Can it be done? _____

3. Cover it using only blue rhombuses. Can it be done? _____

4. Cover it using only triangles. Can it be done? _____

Focal Point

Problem Solving/Geometry – Reinforce relationships among the pattern blocks. Model problems with physical objects.

Materials

- Pattern blocks: red, blue, and green only
- Cube with 6 sides labeled: red, red, blue, blue, green, green
- Game board (student worksheet)

Instructions

Distribute the game board (1 for every 2 players). Explain that the cube is labeled with the same colors as the pattern blocks that are in play (red, blue, and green). Player 1 tosses the cube and selects the block that is the same color as the color indicated on the tossed cube. The block is then placed on any of 3 hexagons labeled "Player 1."

Next, Player 2 tosses the cube, selects the corresponding block, and places it on any of 3 hexagons labeled "Player 2." Players continue taking turns until one player covers all 3 hexagons. If a player cannot use the block tossed, s(he) loses a turn. Have the students play the game 2 or 3 times, alternating who starts.

Guided Learning

After the students have completed the activity, discuss their strategies for covering the hexagons. Ask:

1. Does it matter who goes first? Why or why not?
2. Should you try to cover one hexagon first before covering the remaining hexagons? Why or why not?
3. What are some of the different ways you covered the hexagon?
4. How many triangles cover the hexagon?
5. How many trapezoids cover the hexagon?
6. How many rhombuses cover the hexagon?
7. How many triangles cover the trapezoid?
8. How many triangles cover the rhombus?

Explore More!

Each player covers the first hexagon using only triangles, the second hexagon using only blue rhombuses, and the third hexagon using only trapezoids. Players toss the cube as indicated above, but this time, they remove the block that matches the color tossed. Trades are allowed. (For example, if blue is tossed and the player has no rhombuses left, (s)he can trade a trapezoid for a rhombus and triangle and then remove the rhombus.) The first player with no blocks left is the winner.

© Didax – www.didax.com

Cover Three

Name: _____

(An Activity for 2)

1. **Player 1:** Toss the cube, select the pattern block that matches the color tossed, and place it on any of your 3 hexagons.

2. **Player 2:** Toss the cube, select the appropriate block, and place it on any of your 3 hexagons.

3. Continue to take turns. If one of you cannot use the block indicated by the cube toss, you lose a turn. The first player to cover all 3 hexagons wins.

Player 1

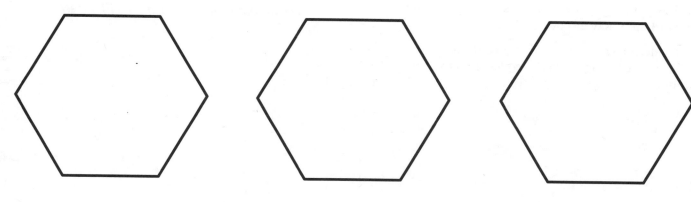

Player 2

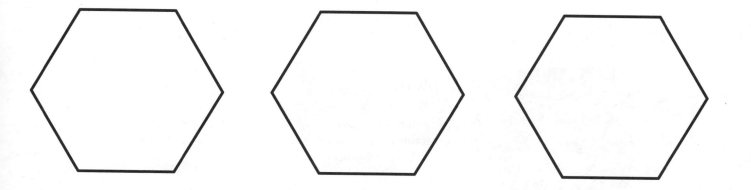

Focal Point

Problem Solving/Representation – Analyze problems by observing patterns. Verify the results of a problem.

Materials

• Pattern blocks

Instructions

Have students cover each hexagon in Tower A in a different way. In covering the hexagons, students may use the same blocks or mix them. Have them record all of their hexagon "discoveries" in Tower B.

Have students remove the blocks and cover each hexagon in Tower A in as many new ways as possible. They then record their new discoveries in Tower C.

(Note: If a design can be rotated and/or flipped to produce another design, it is not considered to be new or different.)

Guided Learning

After the students have placed their arrangements on Tower A, have them sketch their design in Tower B or C before removing the blocks from Tower A. Have them look at two possible hexagon "discoveries" below:

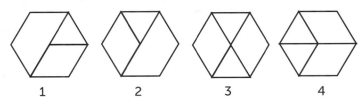

Ask:

1. Are designs #1 and #2 completely different?
   No, if #2 is flipped, you see #1.

2. Are designs #3 and #4 completely different?
   Yes, I can rotate and flip #3, but I will not see #4.

Explore More!

Ask the students: How many different ways to cover the hexagon did you find altogether? Do you think you have found them all? How do you know? Have them justify their solution methods.

Name: _____

1. Cover each hexagon in Tower A in a different way.

2. To cover the hexagons, you may use the same blocks or a combination of different blocks. Sketch your design in Tower B.

3. Remove the blocks and cover each hexagon in Tower A in as many new ways as possible.

4. Sketch your new design in Tower C.

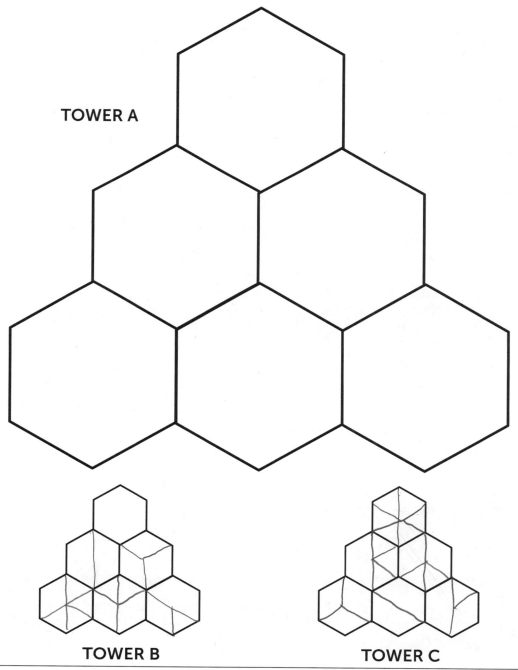

TOWER A

TOWER B   **TOWER C**

Focal Point

Problem Solving/Representation – Solve problems by using guess and check. Use physical objects to model and solve problems. Develop an understanding of equivalences.

Materials

- Pattern blocks
- Triangular grid paper (page 136)

Instructions

Have the students do the following:

1. Use any 6 pattern blocks to completely cover Design #1. Sketch their solution in Figure A.

2. Remove the 6 blocks and select a different combination of 6 blocks. (It's okay to use some of the same blocks again.)

3. Now, completely cover Design #1 again and sketch the second solution in B.

4. Repeat the same procedure for Design #2.

Guided Learning

1. Can you cover the area of Design #1 in more than one way?

2. Which blocks did you use? How was each set of 6 blocks the same? How was each set of 6 different?

3. Compare Figures A and B, and remove the blocks that are the same. (For example, if you remove two triangles from Figure B, you must also remove two triangles from Figure A.) Take the remaining blocks from Figure B and place them on top of the remaining blocks from Figure A. Can you arrange them so they fit exactly?
   Yes

4. Why?

   (If necessary, trade the remaining blocks from Figures A and B for triangles. Is the number of triangles for the two solutions equal?)

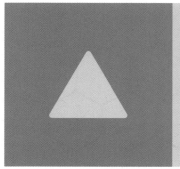

Explore More!

Ask the students: Is it possible to use more than 6 blocks for each design? Have them record their two solutions on triangular grid paper. Is it possible to use fewer than 6 blocks? Have them record their solutions.

What is the difference between the greatest and fewest numbers of blocks needed to complete each design?

© Didax – www.didax.com

Name: _____

Cover each design using only 6 pattern blocks. Can you find another way to cover the design using only 6 blocks? Record your findings in Figures A and B.

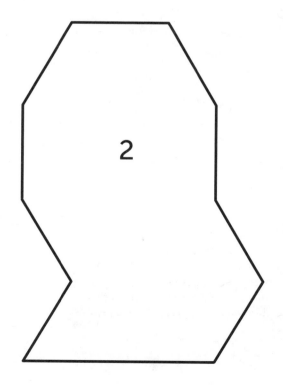

A

B

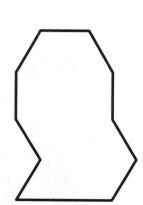

A

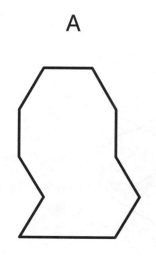

B

© Didax – www.didax.com

Focal Point

Problem Solving/Representation – Model similar designs and replicate patterns with physical objects. Explain methods and reasoning behind problem-solving strategies. Develop visualization skills.

Materials

- Pattern blocks

Instructions

(Note: Designs can be displayed on an overhead projector with transparent pattern blocks.)

Students take the pattern blocks needed to make Design A. Have them move the blocks to the top of their desks but not touch the blocks while they study Design A.

Have the students count backwards from 10 to 1 and turn the page over. Have them recreate the design from memory. Repeat the procedure with Designs B, C, and D.

Guided Learning

1. Which designs were you able to complete from memory?

2. Is it more difficult to reconstruct a design from memory if there are more parts (blocks)?

3. Which designs were easier to recreate?
   A, C
   Why?
   uniform arrangement, symmetry, pattern

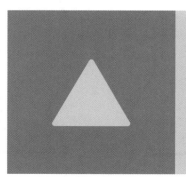

Explore More!

Have the students count from 5 to 1 instead of 10 to 1 and then try to make their design again. Discuss their strategies. Did they focus on color or shape when they were making their design? Why? What else helped them remember the design?

Name: _____

1. Select the pattern blocks you'll need to make one of the designs below.

2. Study the picture and count from 10 to 1.

3. When you reach 1, turn the page over and make the design from memory.

4. Pick another design and try it again!

A.

 **You need 6 blocks**

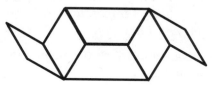

B.

    **You need 6 blocks**

C.

 **You need 7 blocks**

 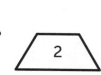 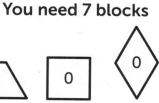

D.

 **You need 11 blocks**

© Didax – www.didax.com

Focal Point

Problem Solving/Representation – Use guess and check to solve problems. Develop visualization skills.

Materials

- Pattern blocks
- Triangular grid paper (page 136)
- Colored pencils or crayons

Instructions

Have students look carefully at grids A, B, C, and D. The indicated blocks fit exactly onto each grid with no overlapping. (Figures are not drawn to scale.)

Using the matching color for each shape, have the students color where each of the indicated blocks fits on the grid.

After they have completed shapes A–D, have them place the corresponding pattern blocks on triangular grid paper to check their solutions. They may correct their sketch, if necessary.

Guided Learning

1. In Hidden Wonder A, which block did you place first? Why?

2. Which blocks did you place first in Hidden Wonders B, C, and D? Why?

   Which pattern blocks are equivalent in area?
   2 triangles = 1 rhombus, 2 trapezoids = 1 hexagon, 1 triangle and 1 rhombus = 1 trapezoid, 3 triangles = 1 trapezoid, 6 triangles = 1 hexagon

3. Why are these equivalent relationships helpful in finding your solutions?

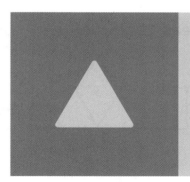

Explore More!

Have the students use pattern blocks to make a hidden wonder that can be covered entirely with 10 trapezoids but not 5 hexagons, and 10 triangles but not 5 rhombuses. Can both of these hidden wonders be made? Why or why not?

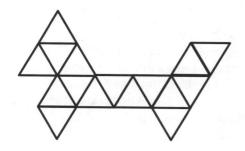

Name: _____

Look carefully at grids A, B, C, and D. The blocks to the right of each grid fit exactly onto the grid with no overlapping.

Color each pattern block on the grid, using the actual color for each shape. Check your solutions using pattern blocks and triangular grid paper.

A.

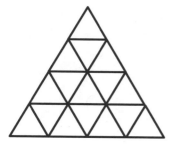

Use only...

B.

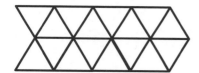

Use only...

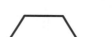

C.

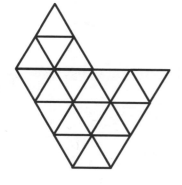

Use only...

D.

Use only...

© Didax – www.didax.com

Focal Point

Problem Solving/Geometry – Solve problems by using guess and check. Introduce and/or reinforce the concept of bilateral symmetry.

Materials

- Pattern blocks
- Ruler

Instructions

Have students take the pattern blocks indicated and make a design (1) that is the same on both sides of the vertical line shown. They may use triangular grid paper to assist them, if necessary. Have the students record their design on the reduced-size grid provided on the worksheet.

Then, have the students make another design (2) that is the same on both sides of a vertical line of their choosing. They record their completed design on the reduced-size grid provided on the activity page. Have them use their ruler to draw a line that shows the design's vertical line of symmetry.

Guided Learning

1. How do you know that Design I is the same on both sides of the vertical line?
   Use the triangular grid on the student page to verify the position of the blocks.

2. Fold your sketch of Design I on the vertical line. What do you see?

Explore More!

Have the students draw a horizontal line on triangular grid paper (page 136). Using 1 hexagon, 4 blue rhombuses, 4 triangles, and 4 trapezoids, have them make a new design that looks the same on both sides of the horizontal line. Tell them to sketch it. Then, have them use the same blocks again and make a design that does not appear to be the same on both sides of the line. Tell them to explain why in writing.

Name: _____

1. Make Design 1 using the pattern blocks shown. It must look the same on both sides of the vertical line of symmetry shown. Sketch the design in the grid provided.

2. Make Design 2 using the pattern blocks shown. This design should also be the same on both sides of a vertical line. Sketch your completed design, and use a ruler to draw the line where the design is the same on both sides.

DESIGN 1

DESIGN 2

Explore & Discover: **Asteroids**

Focal Point

Problem Solving/Geometry – Use physical objects (models) to solve problems. Develop visualization skills. Make predictions.

Materials

- Pattern blocks
- Tape

Instructions

Have students create Asteroids A, B, C, and D using the appropriate pattern blocks and tape.

Students take Asteroid A and rotate it to positions 1, 2, and 3.

Before rotating one more time, they picture what the next position will look like and sketch it in position 4.

They then rotate the asteroid one more time to compare the model to their sketch. Have them make any necessary corrections to their sketch.

They then repeat the process for Asteroids B, C, and D.

Guided Learning

1. Are all the asteroids (A, B, C, and D) rotating clockwise, or are some rotating counterclockwise?

2. When you rotated your asteroids to position 4, did any of them return to their original position?

3. Will any of the asteroids return to position 1 if you rotate them one more time in the same direction (position 5)?

4. Which asteroids look like the original picture when rotated to position 5? *A, B, and C*
   Why?
   They have been turned 360 degrees.

Explore More!

Tell the students that photographs are being taken at 30-second intervals of each position of the asteroids as they rotate in space. Have them assume that the asteroid rotates a quarter-turn every 30 seconds. How much time will elapse before each asteroid returns to its original position?

Have the students make an asteroid that returns to its original position in 3 minutes; in $1\frac{1}{2}$ minutes.

Name: _____

Create the asteroids labeled A, B, C, and D. If necessary, tape the pattern blocks together for asteroids B, C, and D.

Each asteroid is moving through space. Rotate each asteroid to positions 1, 2, and 3, as shown in the pictures.

What would the next picture (position 4) look like? Draw it in the space provided.

1	2	3	4

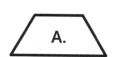

1	2	3	4

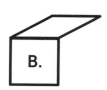

1	2	3	4

1	2	3	4

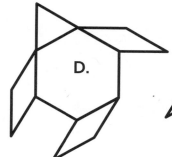

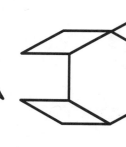

© Didax – www.didax.com

Advanced Pattern Block Book

Number & Operations

Focal Point

Number/Problem Solving – Find solutions using guess and check. Introduce the concept of area equivalence.

Materials

- Pattern blocks

Instructions

Students try to cover each shape on the left using only 4 pattern blocks. The blocks may be the same or different.

When the students have covered the shapes two different ways, have them sketch their designs on the smaller shapes to the right.

Guided Learning

1. Did you find more than two ways to cover a shape?

2. Can you cover any of the shapes using only two kinds of blocks?

Explore More!

Ask the students: Is it possible to cover the shapes using more than 4 blocks for each design? Is it possible to use fewer than 4 blocks? What is the difference between the greatest number of blocks and the fewest number of blocks needed to cover each shape?

Name: _____

1. Cover each shape on the left using any 4 pattern blocks.
2. Try another way using only 4 blocks.
3. Sketch your two designs in Figures A, B, and C.

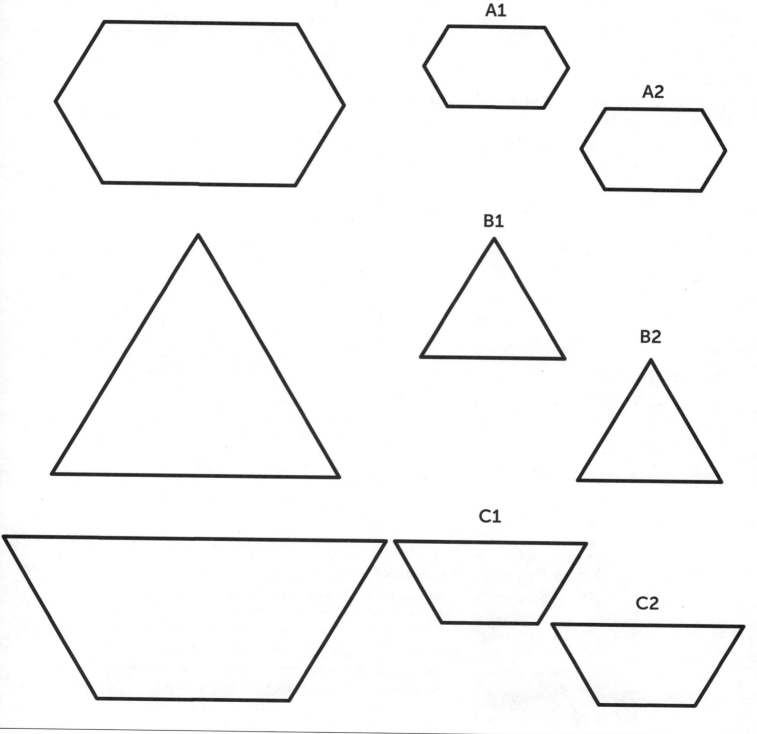

Number & Operations: **The Same Block**

Focal Point

Number/Problem Solving – Find solutions using guess and check. Reinforce the concepts of area equivalence and fractions.

Materials

- Pattern blocks

Instructions

Students try to cover each shape on the left using blocks of the same color only.

When they have covered the shape, they sketch their results in the corresponding figures to the right.

Guided Learning

1. Did you find more than two ways to cover a shape using just one color pattern block?

2. How many of the same blocks did you use in A1? What is the fraction name for each block?

3. How many of the same blocks did you use in A2? What is the fraction name for each block?

Explore More!

Can the students draw a design that can only be covered by blocks of the same color? Ask them to explain in their own words why they think their design works.

Have them look back at their sketch for the first shape in the "Any Four" activity (page 25). What is the fraction name for each piece? Are these equal fractional parts? Why or why not?

     © Didax – www.didax.com

The Same Block

Name: _____

Cover the shape on the left using only pattern blocks of the same color.

Can you find another way to cover the shape using a different-colored pattern block?

Record your findings.

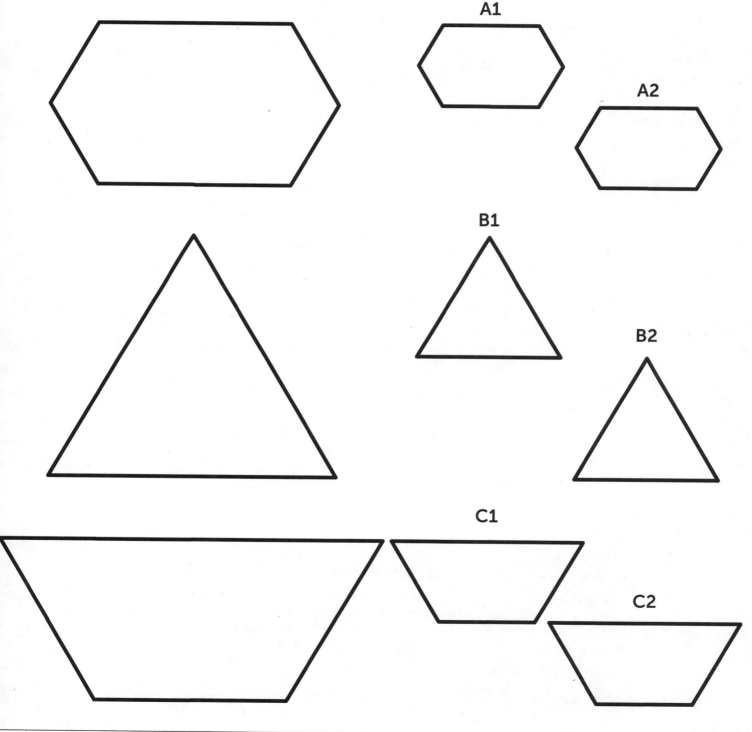

Focal Point

Number/Problem Solving – Investigate relationships among pattern blocks. Practice estimation.

Materials

- Pattern blocks:
  - triangles
  - blue rhombuses
  - trapezoids

Instructions

Students cover designs with specific pattern blocks to begin to understand the relationships among the sizes of the blocks. They also use fractions to name the blocks in relation to each other.

Guided Learning

1. Explain how you estimated the number of blocks needed before covering the design.

2. What is the relationship of the blue rhombus to the green triangle? What is the relationship of the blue rhombus to the trapezoid? Explain your answers.

Explore More!

Ask the students: How many triangles do you need to cover the kite? Can you figure out the answer to the question without covering the design or estimating? Have them explain their method.

© Didax – www.didax.com

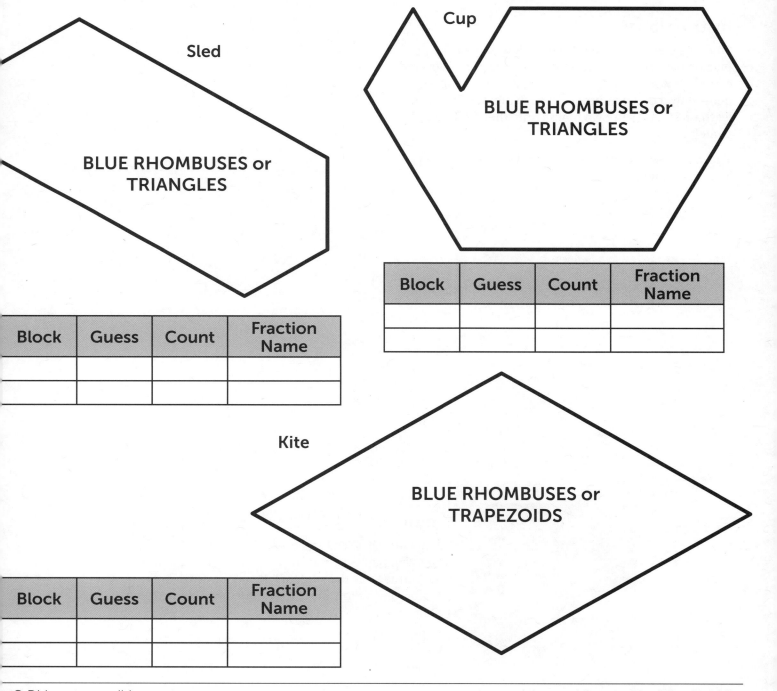

Name: _____

Make each design (sled, cup, kite) using one of the pattern blocks indicated inside its outline.

1. On the table below, guess and record the number of blocks you will need to cover each design without overlapping.
2. Use blocks to find the actual number. Record the actual number in the table.
3. Do the same for the other pattern block indicated inside the outline.
4. Look at the tables and compare your findings. What is the fraction name for each pattern block?

Sled

BLUE RHOMBUSES or TRIANGLES

Cup

BLUE RHOMBUSES or TRIANGLES

Block	Guess	Count	Fraction Name

Block	Guess	Count	Fraction Name

Kite

BLUE RHOMBUSES or TRAPEZOIDS

Block	Guess	Count	Fraction Name

Focal Point

Number/Problem Solving – Use pattern blocks to investigate the relationships among various pattern blocks and to understand equivalence. Use reasoning skills.

Materials

- Pattern blocks

Instructions

Students play the game "Space Station" in pairs by placing pattern blocks on a grid until the grid is covered completely. You can structure the game by giving students only a certain number of each block, or you can let them chose their own blocks until they find a good strategy.

The last person to place a block on the Space Station loses the game.

Guided Learning

1. Which shapes are the easiest to place? Which seem to be the hardest?

2. If you have a rule that the next shape placed must touch another shape on the grid, is the game more difficult?

3. If the hexagon is equal to one, what is the fractional value of each of the pieces? Think: how many triangles does the hexagon cover on the grid?

Explore More!

Change the rules. The students play as above, but the player who places the last block on the Space Station is the winner. Ask the students: If you play with only red, blue, and yellow pieces, how does that change your strategy? Can you cover the grid?

© Didax – www.didax.com

Space Station

![trapezoid logo]

Name: _____

(An Activity for 2)

Player 1: Place a pattern block anywhere on the Space Station so that it covers one or more triangles completely.

Player 2: Select a block and do the same.

Continue to take turns until no more blocks can be placed on the Space Station.

The player who places the last block on the Space Station loses the game.

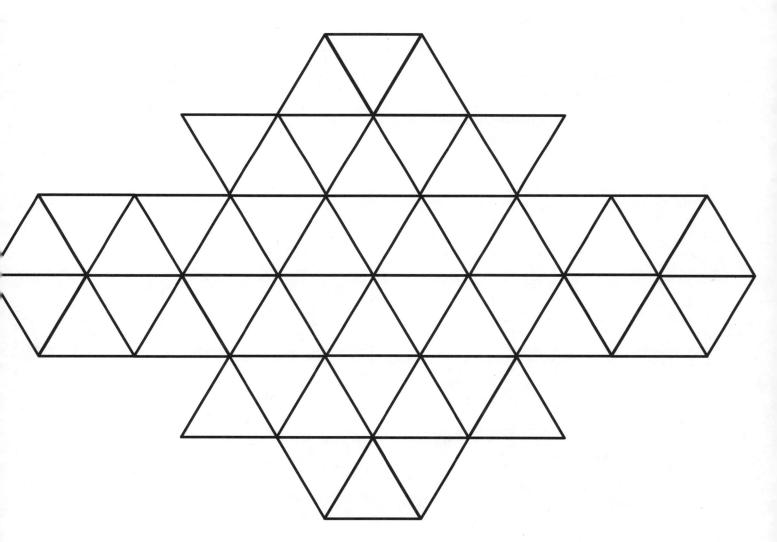

Focal Point

Number Sense/Representation – Review relationships among pattern blocks using physical objects as representations. Develop the concept of fractions.

Materials

- Pattern blocks

Instructions

Ask students to recall the "Space Station" activity (page 31) and how many triangles were covered by the hexagon, trapezoid, and blue rhombus.

Reinforce the fraction name of these blocks when the hexagon equals one whole unit.

In this activity, students take the pattern blocks indicated by their fraction name (for example, $\frac{2}{3}$) and trace the shape in the space provided.

Guided Learning

Fill in the three blanks at the beginning of Part B together. Ask students to identify the shaded and unshaded areas of the hexagons in Exercises 1–5 using the appropriate fraction name.

Reinforce students' understanding that when the two areas are put together (unshaded and shaded), you have one whole unit.

Ask: In each example, which is greater: the shaded or unshaded fractional part?

Explore More!

Have the students find other fraction names for one whole unit. $\frac{2}{2}$, $\frac{3}{3}$, $\frac{6}{6}$, *and so on*

Have them represent the following fraction names with pattern blocks: $2\frac{1}{3}$, $1\frac{3}{6}$, $1\frac{1}{6}$, $2\frac{2}{3}$, $3\frac{1}{2}$. Then, ask them to arrange these fractions from smallest to greatest. Tell them to justify their answer using pattern blocks.

Name: _____

A. Assume the hexagon has a value of one whole unit. Use pattern blocks to outline the shapes that represent the fraction names below.

$\frac{2}{3}$ $\frac{4}{6}$

$1\frac{1}{2}$ $\frac{5}{6}$

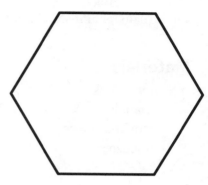

B. Fill in the blanks. As you can see, if the hexagon equals one whole unit, then the trapezoid equals _____, the rhombus equals _____, and the triangle equals _____.

Find the fraction names for the shaded and unshaded areas.

1. EXAMPLE: ___$\frac{1}{2}$___ shaded   ___$\frac{1}{2}$___ unshaded

2.   _____ shaded   _____ unshaded

3.   _____ shaded   _____ unshaded

4.   _____ shaded   _____ unshaded

5.   _____ shaded   _____ unshaded

Focal Point

Number/Connections – Develop the concept of one (whole) with fractions using physical objects to explore and explain relationships among mathematical ideas.

Materials

* Pattern blocks:
  * triangles
  * blue rhombuses
  * trapezoids

Instructions

Have the students use only the following pattern blocks: trapezoids, blue rhombuses, and triangles. Guide them through the exercises on the worksheet, as follows:

1. Have them cover the hexagon first with only trapezoids. Ask: How many trapezoids did you need?

2. Point out that since only 2 trapezoids were needed, each trapezoid is one of two trapezoids needed (or $\frac{1}{2}$ of the hexagon). Have them fill in the blanks on the activity page for question 1.

3. Have the students do the same with the blue rhombuses and triangles (questions 2 and 3).

4. For question 4, say: Now we are going to find the one missing pattern block that will make 1 (the whole hexagon). Let's do the first one together. Place 1 trapezoid and then 1 rhombus in the hexagon at the top of the page. What one block is needed to complete the figure and make 1 (the hexagon)? *1 triangle* What is its fractional name in relation to 1 (the whole hexagon)? *Answer:* $\frac{1}{6}$

5. Have the students complete exercises 5–8. In 9–13, the fractional names are given. The students place the corresponding blocks on the hexagon to find out which fractional part is missing.

Guided Learning

1. How many trapezoids cover the 1 (hexagon)? Each is therefore _____ of the hexagon.

2. How many blue rhombuses cover the 1 (hexagon)? Each is therefore _____ of the hexagon.

3. How many triangles cover the 1 (hexagon)? Each is therefore _____ of the hexagon.

4. How many $\frac{1}{2}$'s equal 1?

5. How many $\frac{1}{3}$'s equal 1?

6. How many $\frac{1}{6}$'s equal 1"

7. The sum $\frac{1}{6} + \frac{1}{3} + \frac{1}{2}$ equals what number?
   1
   Explain.

Explore More!

To do the following exercises, the students will need 2 blocks of the same kind to make 1 (whole hexagon). Which kind of block is needed?

2 blue rhombuses + _____ = 1 (whole hexagon)   *2 triangles*

$\frac{1}{2} + \frac{1}{6} +$ _____ = 1 (whole hexagon)   *2 triangles*

$\frac{3}{6} + \frac{1}{6} +$ _____ = 1 (whole hexagon)   *2 triangles*

Have students explain why all the examples need 2 triangles. Have them write the explanation in their math journal.

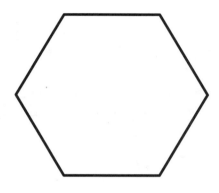

Just One (Hexagon)!

Name: _____

Follow the directions and fill in the blanks.

1. Cover the hexagon with only trapezoids. Since _____ trapezoids cover the hexagon, each trapezoid is _____ of the hexagon.

2. Cover the hexagon with only blue rhombuses. Since _____ blue rhombuses cover the hexagon, each rhombus is _____ of the hexagon.

3. Cover the hexagon with only triangles. Since _____ triangles cover the hexagon, each triangle is _____ of the hexagon.

Place the indicated pattern blocks in the outline of the hexagon above to find the block(s) that will make just one hexagon. Write the name of the missing block and its fraction name in the spaces provided.

4. 1 trapezoid + 1 rhombus + $\underset{\textit{(missing block)}}{\underline{\text{1 triangle}}}$ [$\underset{\substack{\textit{(fraction} \\ \textit{name)}}}{\frac{1}{6}}$] = 1 (whole hexagon)

5. 2 rhombuses + 1 triangle + _____ [ ] = 1 (whole hexagon)

6. 1 trapezoid + 1 triangle + _____ [ ] = 1 (whole hexagon)

7. 3 triangles + _____ [ ] = 1 (whole hexagon)

8. 2 triangles + 1 rhombus + _____ [ ] = 1 (whole hexagon)

9. $\frac{1}{6} + \frac{1}{3} +$ _____ [ ] = 1 (whole hexagon)

10. $\frac{2}{6} + \frac{1}{3} +$ _____ [ ] = 1 (whole hexagon)

11. $\frac{1}{3} + \frac{1}{2} +$ _____ [ ] = 1 (whole hexagon)

12. $\frac{1}{3} + \frac{1}{3} +$ _____ [ ] = 1 (whole hexagon)

13. $\frac{1}{3} + \frac{3}{6} +$ _____ [ ] = 1 (whole hexagon)

© Didax – www.didax.com

Focal Point

Number Sense/Representation – Develop the concept of equivalence. Use representations to explore problem situations and develop the concept of addition of fractions.

Materials

- Pattern blocks

Instructions

Have the students cover each design (A–F) with the pattern blocks indicated. Students will use same-color pattern blocks for each design. Assuming the hexagon represents one whole unit, have them write the fraction name for the original design and the equivalent fraction name (for the covering pieces) in the form of a number sentence.

Guided Learning

Reinforce the understanding that fractional numbers, like whole numbers, have many names for the same value.

Ask: What one pattern block covers 3 triangles? If the hexagon = 1, what is another name for $\frac{3}{6}$? *Answer:* $\frac{1}{2}$

What one pattern block covers 1 triangle and 1 blue rhombus? If a hexagon = 1, what is another name for $\frac{1}{6} + \frac{1}{3}$? *Answer:* $\frac{1}{2}$

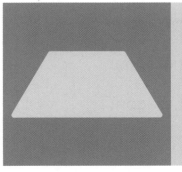

Explore More!

Have the students make three new and original examples of equivalence, as follows: Take two or more pattern blocks, put them together, and outline the resulting shape. Find the same-color pattern block that will cover the area of the new shape. Write the corresponding addition sentence.

© Didax – www.didax.com

Name: _____

Cover each design with the pattern blocks shown below.

Find the equivalent values by placing pattern blocks (of one color) on top of each design. Compare each pattern block to the hexagon (one whole unit) and record each fraction name.

Write a number sentence showing the fraction names and the equivalent values. (See Example A.)

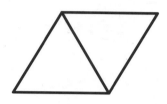

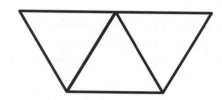

A. $\dfrac{1}{6} + \dfrac{1}{6} = \dfrac{1}{3}$ _____

B. _____

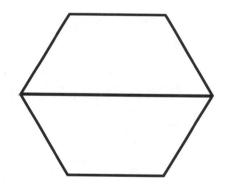

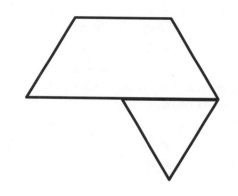

C. _____

D. _____

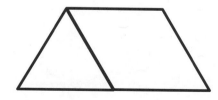

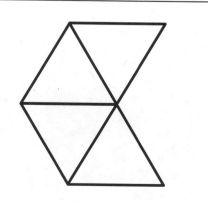

E. _____

F. _____

Focal Point

Number Sense/Representation – Develop proportional relationships. Reinforce the concept of missing addends. Develop visualization and estimation skills.

Materials

- Pattern blocks

Instructions

Have the students cover the hexagonal design at the top of the worksheet with hexagons only, then trapezoids only, then blue rhombuses only, and finally triangles only.

Tell them that in each exercise there is a missing pattern block that they will need to cover the design completely. Have them take the blocks indicated but first guess which block is missing. Then have them place the pattern blocks indicated in the hexagonal design at the top of the page, identify the missing block, and record its fraction name.

Remind students that the fraction names for triangles, blue rhombuses, and trapezoids will change when two hexagons equal one whole unit.

Guided Learning

1. What are the fraction names of the triangle, blue rhombus, and trapezoid in this activity?
   Answer: $\frac{1}{12}$, $\frac{1}{6}$, $\frac{1}{4}$
   How have the fraction names changed?

2. What is the value in each exercise when you add the missing piece to the pattern blocks indicated? *1*

Explore More!

Have the students create two exercises of their own using three different pattern blocks for the two-hexagonal design. Ask students to explain in writing why the fraction names of the pattern blocks may change in different activities.

© Didax – www.didax.com

The Missing Piece

Name: _____

In each of the exercises below, 2 hexagons equal one whole unit.

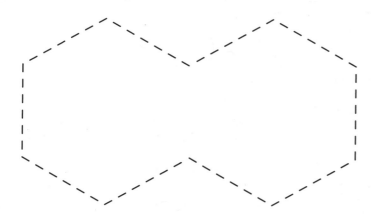

Fill in the design with the pattern blocks indicated. Then find the missing block(s) that will make one whole unit.

Give the fraction name for the missing block. See Example 1 below.

PATTERN BLOCKS	SHADED AREA	MISSING BLOCK	FRACTION NAME
1. 2 trapezoids + 2 blue rhombuses		+ blue rhombus = 1	$\frac{1}{6}$
2. 3 trapezoids + 1 triangle		+	= 1
3. 1 hexagon + 2 triangles		+	= 1
4. 1 trapezoid + 1 triangle + 1 blue rhombus		+	= 1
5. 2 blue rhombuses + 2 triangles		+	= 1
6. 3 triangles + 3 blue rhombuses		+	= 1

Number & Operations: **Some Sum!**

Focal Point

Number Sense/Representation/Problem Solving –
Develop the concept of equivalence. Use various
strategies to add fractions together.

Materials

- Pattern blocks
- Triangular grid paper (page 136)

Instructions

Have students read the directions at the top of the page
carefully. Ask them why the fraction names for the pattern blocks are different from those in activities such as
Space Station.

Model Exercise 1 on an overhead projector, if available.
Ask students to take pattern blocks representing $\frac{1}{12} + \frac{1}{12}$
and place them on the hexagonal design at the top of
the page. Then have them find one block that will cover
the remaining area completely. Ask: What is its fraction
name? Have the students complete Exercises 2–6.

Guided Learning

1. Which exercises have the same fraction value for the
   answer? Why?

2. What two fractions can you name that will cover the
   entire area?

3. What are other names for 1? *Answer:* $\frac{2}{2}, \frac{4}{4}, \frac{6}{6}, \frac{12}{12}, \ldots$

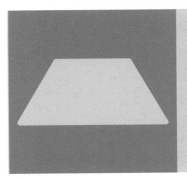

Explore More!

Have the students arrange the following fractions from
smallest to largest. To check their answer, have them
model each fraction by placing the appropriate pattern
blocks on the two-hexagonal design (equal to 1 unit).
Then, have them illustrate the following fractions on
triangular grid paper: $\frac{2}{2}, \frac{1}{6}, \frac{3}{4}, \frac{6}{12}, \frac{3}{12}$

    © Didax – www.didax.com

Some Sum!

Name: _____

If 2 hexagons together equal 1 whole unit, the hexagon equals $\frac{1}{2}$, the trapezoid equals $\frac{1}{4}$, the blue rhombus equals $\frac{1}{6}$, and the triangle equals $\frac{1}{12}$.

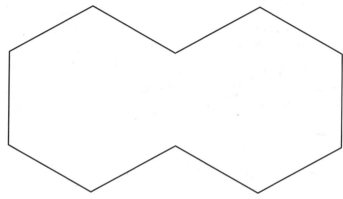

1. Take the blocks indicated by their fraction name and place them in the outline at the left.

2. Find the one-color equivalent block or blocks.

3. Complete the table below as shown in examples 1 and 2.

		NUMBER VALUE
1. $\frac{1}{12} + \frac{1}{12} =$	= 1 triangle + 1 triangle = 1 blue rhombus =	_____
2. $\frac{1}{2} + \frac{1}{4} =$	= 1 hexagon + 1 trapezoid = 3 trapezoids =	_____
3. $\frac{1}{12} + \frac{1}{6} =$	=	_____
4. $\frac{1}{6} + \frac{2}{6} =$	=	_____
5. $\frac{4}{12} + \frac{1}{6} =$	=	_____
6. $\frac{1}{4} + \frac{3}{6} =$	=	_____

© Didax – www.didax.com

Focal Point

Number Sense/Representation – Use various strategies to add fractions with like and unlike denominators. Continue to develop the concept of equivalence.

Materials

- Pattern blocks

Instructions

Have the students cover the outline at the top of the page with hexagons only. Ask: What is the fraction name for one hexagon? Have the students do the same for the other pattern blocks shown at the top of the page. Have them write the fraction name for the pattern blocks in the spaces provided.

Model Example 1, placing the two trapezoids in the outline at the top of the page. Place one hexagon on top of the two trapezoids to show it covers the same area completely. Ask: What is another name for $\frac{1}{4} + \frac{1}{4}$?

Next, have the students model Exercise 1 as you observe them. Then have them complete Exercises 2–8.

Guided Learning

Explain that when two or more fractions cover the same area as another fraction ($\frac{2}{4} = \frac{1}{2}$), we say the fractions are equivalent. Equivalent fractions are equal in area.

Ask students to look at Exercises 1–8 to find the many different fractions that are equal to $\frac{1}{2}$.

Write these sentences together and compare the fraction names that are the same and different in each number sentence.

Explore More!

Have the students create three examples of their own whose sum equals $\frac{3}{4}$. Have them use pattern blocks to check their work. Tell them to explain in writing the similarities and differences between the addends in each number sentence.

Name: _____

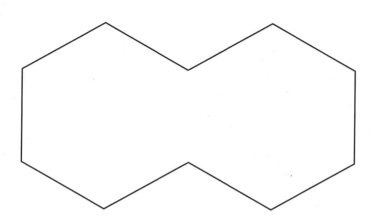

If the hexagonal design on the left represents one whole unit, then indicate the fraction name of each of the following.

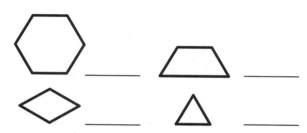

In each exercise, look at the shaded area and duplicate it in the two-hexagon outline above. Then find an equivalent value for the shaded area by placing different pattern blocks (of one color) on top of those blocks.

Record the fraction name of each block in the design and the new equivalent value in a number sentence. (See Example 1.)

1.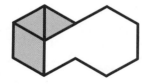

$\frac{1}{4} + \frac{1}{4} = \frac{1}{2}$

_____

2.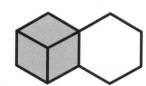

_____

3.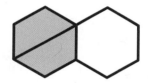

_____

4.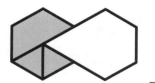

_____

5.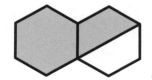

_____

6.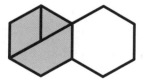

_____

7.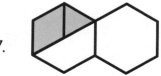

_____

8.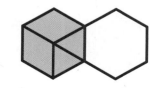

_____

© Didax – www.didax.com

Advanced Pattern Block Book

Geometry

Focal Point

Geometry/Reasoning and Proof – Classify polygons by properties of their angles and sides. Use various types of reasoning and methods of proof. Use representations to organize, record, and communicate ideas.

Materials

• Pattern blocks

Instructions

Take one each of the 6 pattern blocks pictured. Notice the number of sides and kinds of angles on each pattern block as your finger traces each shape's perimeter. Read the clues in A, B, and C to determine which pattern block is indicated. Use a matrix or any other strategy in Problem D to match a pattern block to a person.

Guided Learning

1. Which blocks have acute, obtuse, or right angles?

2. Which blocks have only angles of the same measure?

3. Which blocks are quadrilaterals?

4. Which blocks have at least one pair of parallel lines?

5. Which blocks are parallelograms?

Explore More!

Have the students write their own pattern block riddles. Have them write one that can be answered with three clues and one that needs four clues. Have them ask another student to solve their riddles.

Name: _____

1. Blocks were placed in a box. Frances put her hand inside the box, picked a block, and described it. She did this 3 times. Guess which block she picked each time.

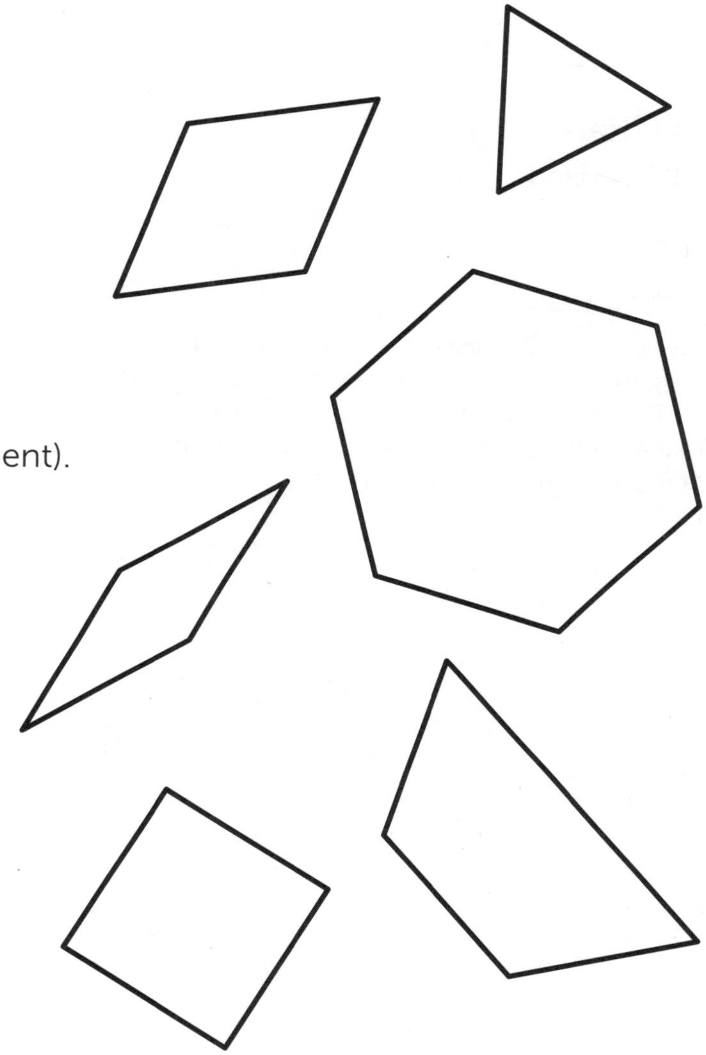

A. Frances's first pick:

It has four sides.
It has obtuse and acute angles.
Only one pair of opposite sides is parallel.

Which block is it? _____

B. Frances's second pick:

It has fewer than 6 sides.
All of its sides are of equal measure (congruent).
It has no right angles.

Which block is it? _____

C. Frances's third pick:

It has more than one line of symmetry.
It has more than 3 sides.
It has obtuse angles.
It's not a parallelogram.

Which block is it? _____

2. Maggie, Bill, Vincent, and Sandi each selected a different pattern block. Maggie's block had all sides and angles of equal measure. Bill's block had obtuse and acute angles. One of the blocks had only 3 sides. Vincent's block had just one line of symmetry. Sandi's block had an area equivalent to 2 triangles. Who had which block?

Maggie: _____

Bill: _____

Vincent: _____

Sandi: _____

Geometry: **Folded Shapes**

Focal Point

Geometry/Representation – Review the concept of symmetry. Draw the image of a figure under a reflection of a given line. Use representations to explore mathematical concepts.

Materials

- Pattern blocks
- Triangular grid paper (page 136)

Instructions

Have the students place the pattern blocks as pictured in Figure 1. This design was folded along the indicated line of symmetry. Have the students imagine what each design would look like unfolded and then have them sketch it. Have them use the pattern blocks to complete the "unfolded" design. They then compare the unfolded design to their sketch. Have them repeat the process for Figures 2, 3, and 4.

Guided Learning

1. Which design was the most difficult to construct? Why?

2. Which designs have vertical symmetry? Horizontal symmetry?

3. Which designs have more than one line of symmetry?

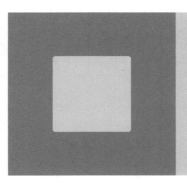

Explore More!

Using pattern blocks, have each student make an original design that has two lines of symmetry. Have them imagine it folded along either line of symmetry and record the result. They should ask another student to build the original design from their sketch of the folded figure.

© Didax – www.didax.com

Folded Shapes

Name: _____

These pattern block designs were folded along the indicated line of symmetry. Imagine what each design would like unfolded, and sketch it. Check your thinking by using the pattern blocks to copy the figure and build the symmetrical design.

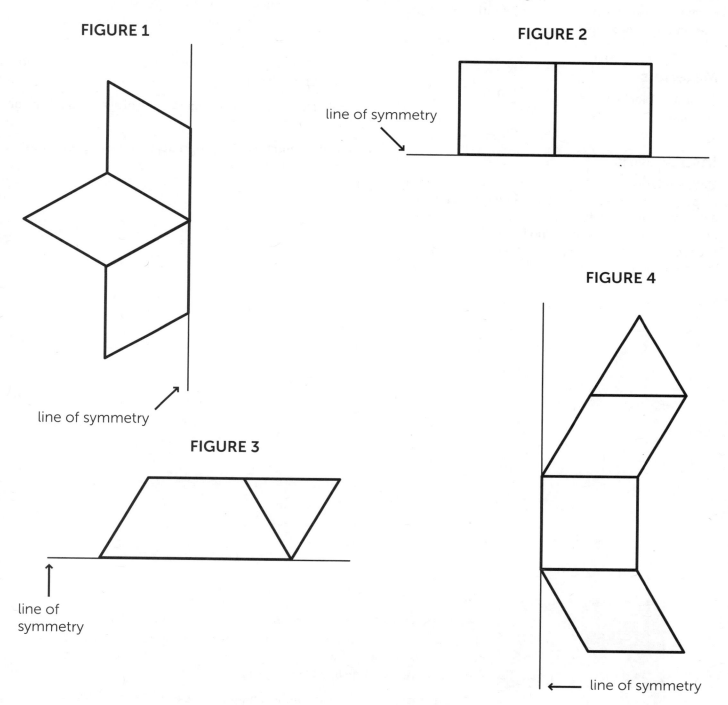

FIGURE 1

line of symmetry

FIGURE 2

line of symmetry

FIGURE 3

line of symmetry

FIGURE 4

line of symmetry

Which designs have more than one line of symmetry? _____

Geometry: **Simple Symmetry**

Focal Point

Geometry/Representation – Continue to develop the concept of bilateral symmetry. Introduce the concept of rotational symmetry. Use representations to explore mathematical concepts.

Materials

- Pattern blocks
- Ruler

Instructions

Have students use pattern blocks to cover the rocket ship. Have them sketch the blocks they used and draw a line of symmetry with a ruler. If the pattern block arrangement they made has no line of symmetry, have them cover the rocket ship again so that there is a line of symmetry. Repeat the process for the remaining figures.

Guided Learning

1. Do all four figures have at least one line of symmetry? Show them.

2. How can you cover the rocket ship, the kite, and the sailboat so that they have at least one line of symmetry (bilateral)?

3. How can you cover the shapes so that there are no lines of symmetry?

4. Does the pinwheel have a line of symmetry? Why or why not?

Note: Point out, if appropriate, that the pinwheel has rotational symmetry

Explore More!

Have the students cover the figures on the activity page another way, if possible. Do the lines of symmetry change? Using different blocks, can they still have the same line of symmetry?

Tell students to take one each of the 6 pattern blocks. Have them draw the line(s) of symmetry for each kind of block. Which block has the most lines of symmetry?

   © Didax – www.didax.com

Name: _____

Use pattern blocks to cover each figure below. Sketch the blocks you used. Draw all the lines of symmetry.

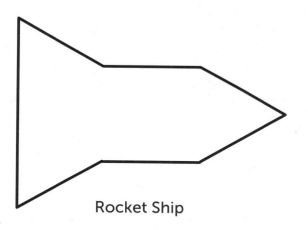

Rocket Ship

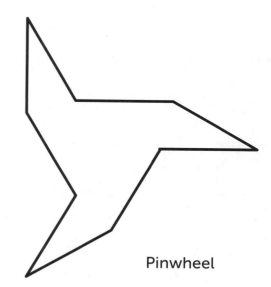

Pinwheel

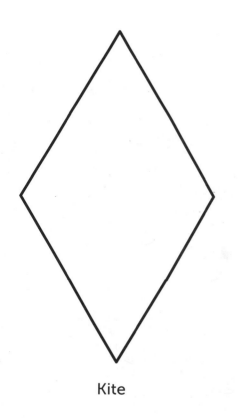

Kite

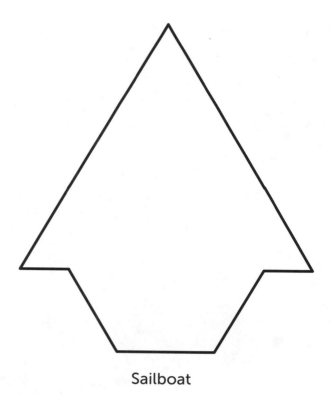

Sailboat

Focal Point

Geometry/Representation – Construct images of a figure under the reflection of a given line (mirror image). Use representations to explore problem situations.

Materials

- Pattern blocks
- Small mirrors

Instructions

Have the students do the following:

1. Look at Design A and imagine they are seeing it in a mirror.

2. Take the pattern blocks they will need to cover the design completely.

3. Build the reflected image of the design to create a mirror image and then use a mirror to check the image. Record what they have built in the column on the right side of the worksheet.

4. Complete Designs B and C.

Guided Learning

1. For which design was it easiest to find the mirror image? Why?

2. Do Designs A, B, and C have horizontal or vertical lines of symmetry?

3. How do lines of symmetry help (or not help) you find a reflected (mirror) image?

Explore More!

Have the students make a design and sketch it. Have them ask another student to copy their design as if he or she were seeing it in a mirror.

© Didax – www.didax.com

Name: _____

Look at Designs A, B, and C. Build each one as if you were seeing it in a mirror. Use a mirror to check what you've built. Then record what you've built. The first one has been started for you.

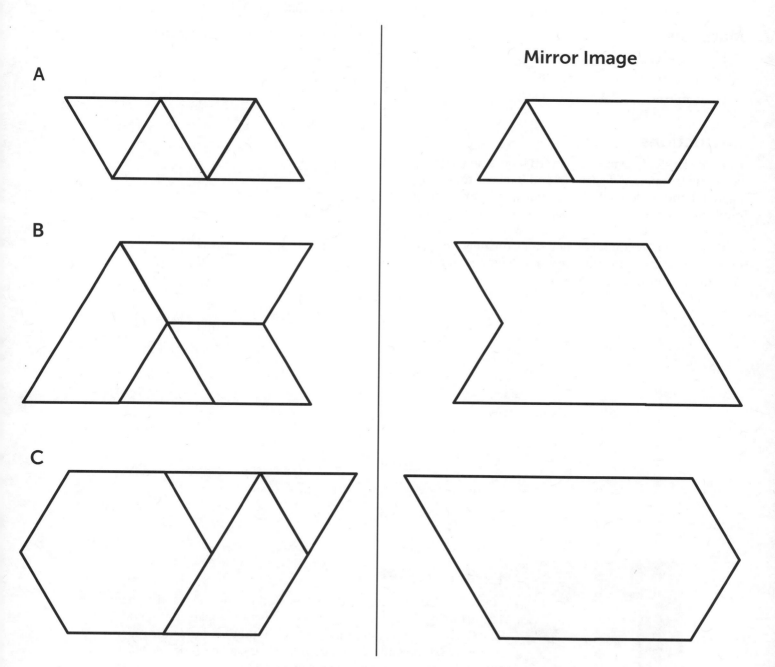

Mirror Image

A

B

C

Focal Point

Geometry/Representation – Continue to develop the concept of reflected (mirror) images. Use representation as a tool for exploring and understanding mathematical ideas.

Materials

- Pattern blocks
- Triangular grid paper (page 136)
- Small mirrors

Instructions

Have the students place the pattern blocks needed to cover the first pair of designs (A and B) at the top of the page. Tell the students that each pair was a mirror image until some of the blocks in Design B were changed. Have them rearrange the blocks in Design B so that it is a mirror image of A. Students then draw the new Design B on triangular grid paper and repeat the process for the second and third pair of designs.

Guided Learning

1. Are any of the blocks in Design B different from those in Design A? *No*

2. Which pattern blocks were reflected correctly?

3. Which blocks, if any, remained in the same place when reflected? Why?

4. How many pattern blocks were changed in Design B?

Explore More!

Have the students choose one of the outlines on the activity page. Using the indicated pattern blocks, have them make another design that fits the outline. How many ways can they scramble the pieces within the same outline? Tell them to sketch all their designs on triangular grid paper and then sketch their mirror images. Have them compare their work with a partner's.

© Didax – www.didax.com

Scrambled Images

Name: _____

Place the indicated pattern blocks on each pair of designs below. Each pair was a mirror image until some of the blocks in Design B were scrambled. Rearrange the blocks in Design B to make the mirror image of Design A. Draw the new Design B on triangular grid paper.

Design A   **Design B**

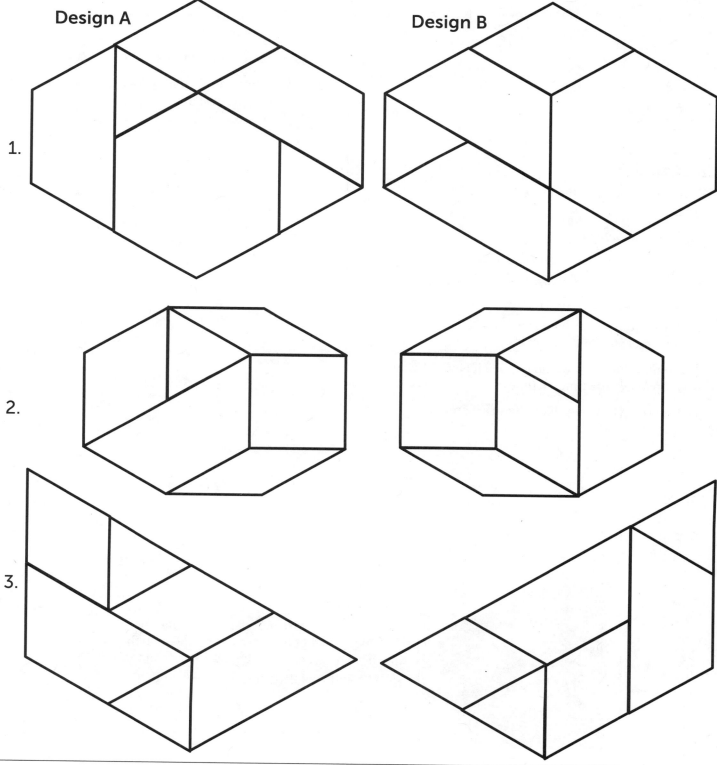

1.

2.

3.

Focal Point

Geometry/Representation – Draw images of a reflection over a given line. Develop an understanding of how different representations express the same relationship —for example, a vertical flip and a reflection both produce a mirror image.

Materials

- Pattern blocks
- Small mirrors

Instructions

Have the students do the following:

1. Take the pattern blocks needed to cover Figure A exactly as shown.

2. Imagine what Figure A would look like if it were flipped once along the indicated line.

3. Sketch it in the outline provided.

4. Check your sketch with a mirror placed along the line indicated in Figure A.

5. Think about what would happen if Figure A were flipped twice, 5 times, 8 times.

6. Complete 1 through 5 for Figures B and C.

Guided Learning

1. What happened when a figure was flipped twice?

2. What happened when a figure was flipped an even number of times?

3. What happened when a figure was flipped an odd number of times?

4. What pattern did you see?

5. What other transformation can produce the same result as a vertical flip?
   Reflection

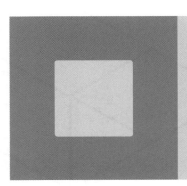

Explore More!

Have the students construct a figure that does not change when it is flipped. Have them explain in their math journal why it does not change. Tell them to sketch the figure and indicate how it was flipped.

© Didax – www.didax.com

The Flip Side

Name: _____

Use pattern blocks to copy each figure. What would each figure look like if it were flipped once along the indicated line? Sketch it in the outline provided.

What would it look like if it were flipped twice? Five times? Eight times? Is there a pattern? Does it always work?

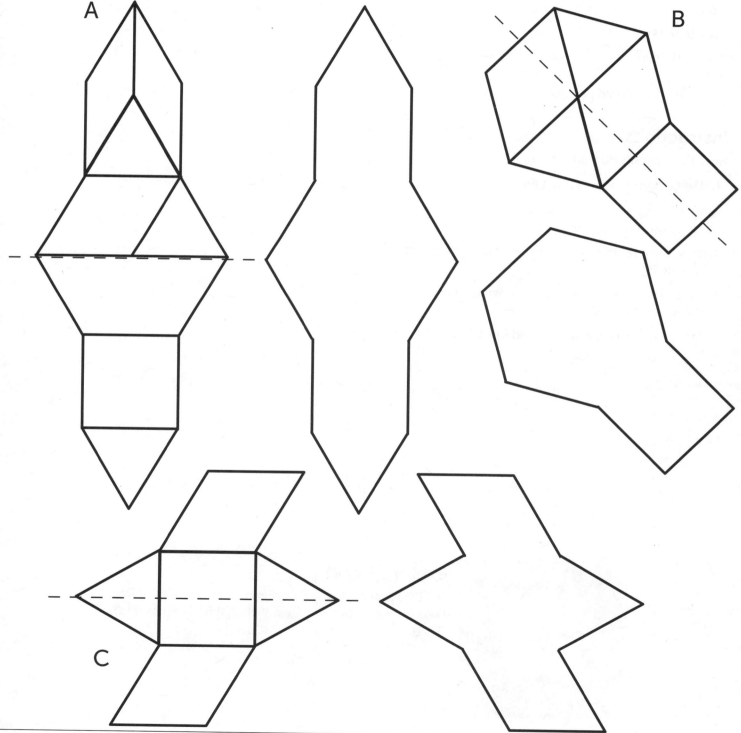

Focal Point

Geometry/Representation – Apply transformations and symmetry to analyze problem-solving situations. Investigate relationships between different representations and their impact on a given problem.

Materials

- Pattern blocks
- Tape
- Crayons or colored pencils

Instructions

Have the students do the following:

1. Use pattern blocks to build the first figure.

2. Imagine what it would look like if it were flipped along the indicated line.

3. Tape the pattern blocks together, if necessary, and flip the figure.

4. Record your results in the grid provided using crayons or colored pencils.

5. Do the same for the second and third figures.

Guided Learning

1. Which flips are easier to picture (those along horizontal lines or vertical lines)? Why?

2. What transformation produces the same result as a flip?

Explore More!

Tell the students to flip each figure about a different line and compare it to the original figure. What do they find?

© Didax – www.didax.com

The Flip Side One More Time

Name: _____

Use pattern blocks to build each figure. What would each figure look like if it were flipped once along the indicated line?

Sketch and color the flip side in the grid provided.

A

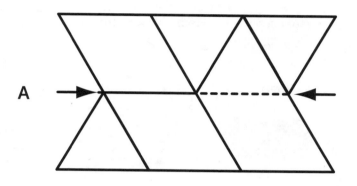 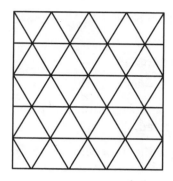

B

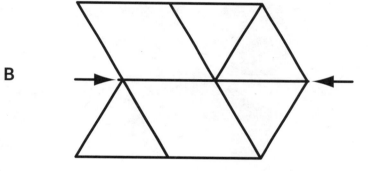 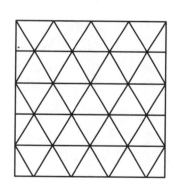

C

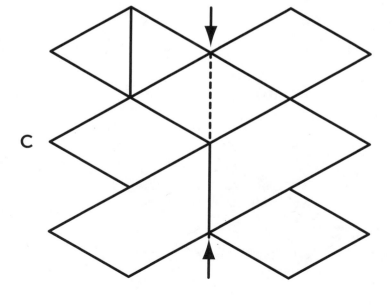 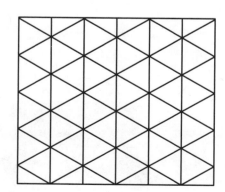

Focal Point

Geometry/Representation – Explore rotational symmetry. Draw the image of a figure under rotations of 90, 180, and 270 degrees.

Materials

- Pattern blocks

Instructions

Have the students do the following:

1. Look at the example and place the trapezoid where indicated.

2. Rotate the trapezoid clockwise in a one-quarter turn (90 degrees), two-quarters or a half turn (180 degrees), and three-quarters (270 degrees).

3. For each of the quarter-turns, copy the resulting figure on the grid provided.

4. Do the same for the three other figures.

Guided Learning

1. In the trapezoid example, what other transformation is the same as a half-turn?
   Reflection or flip horizontally

2. Does that occur for the other three figures? Why or why not?

3. What happens if you make one more quarter-turn for each figure (a four-quarters turn, or 360 degrees)?
   The figure turns to its original position.

Answers

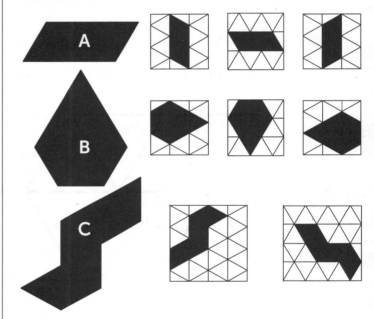

Explore More!

Have the students make a design that looks the same, no matter which turn (quarter, half, or three-quarter) they make.

Turn About

© Didax — www.didax.com

Name: _____

Rotate each design clockwise the indicated amount. Copy the resulting figure on the small grid.

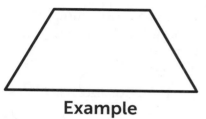

Example

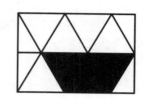

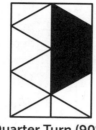
Quarter Turn (90°)

Half Turn (180°)

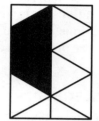
Three-quarter Turn (270°)

A

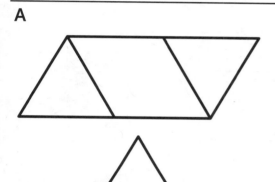

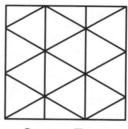
Quarter Turn

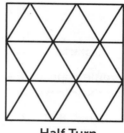
Half Turn

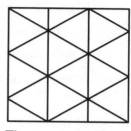
Three-quarter Turn

B

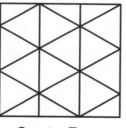
Quarter Turn

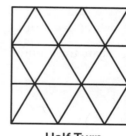
Half Turn

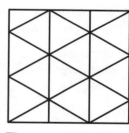
Three-quarter Turn

C

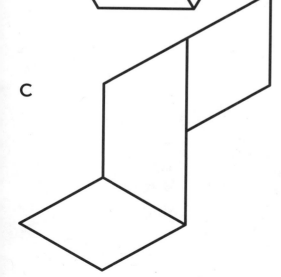

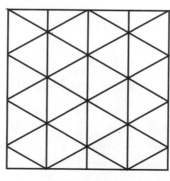
Half Turn

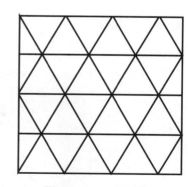
Three-quarter Turn

Focal Point

Geometry/Representation – Continue to apply transformations and symmetry to analyze problem-solving situations. Use visualization and spatial reasoning to analyze properties of geometric figures.

Materials

- Pattern blocks

Instructions

Have students do the following:

1. Look at the first figure and its parts.

2. Visualize how the figure would appear after a three-quarter, or 270-degree, rotation clockwise.

3. Shade the figure on the grid provided.

4. Check their prediction using the indicated pattern blocks.

5. Follow the same procedure for the second figure after a one-quarter, or 90-degree, rotation.

6. For the last two figures, indicate the amount they may have been rotated.

Guided Learning

1. Which turn was easier to visualize—a 270-degree rotation or a 90-degree rotation?

2. Instead of making a three-quarter turn, or 270-degree rotation, clockwise, what other type of rotation would be the same?
   One-quarter turn counterclockwise

3. Which would be easier to visualize? Why?

Answers

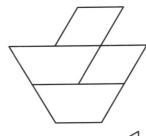

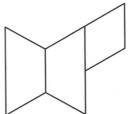

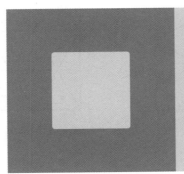

Explore More!

Have the students create a figure that looks the same as the original when it is rotated 180 degrees or 360 degrees, but looks different after a 90- or 270-degree rotation. Have them record both their figure and its rotations in their math journal.

© Didax – www.didax.com

One Good Turn Deserves Another

Name: _____

Predict how the figure would appear when rotated as indicated in a clockwise direction. Shade the resulting figure on the grid. Use pattern blocks to check your prediction.

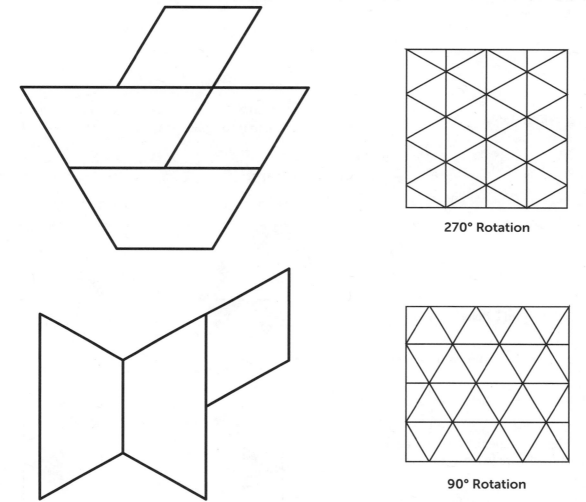

270° Rotation

90° Rotation

For each figure, indicate the amount it has been rotated clockwise.

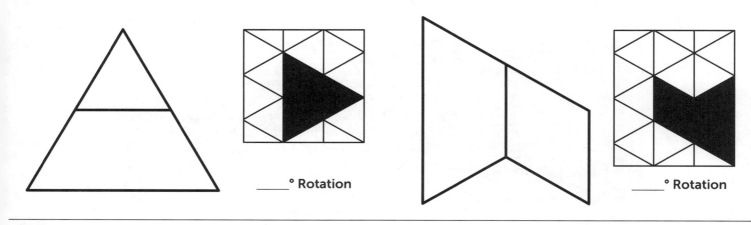

_____° Rotation

_____° Rotation

Focal Point

Geometry/Representation – Continue to develop the concept of reflection and rotation. Use representations to solve problems.

Materials

- Pattern blocks
- Triangular grid paper (page 136)
- Small mirrors
- Tape

Instructions

Have students do the following:

1. Place the pattern blocks as shown in the first figure.

2. Imagine the figure is reflected as indicated by Horizontal Line 1.

3. Sketch the results on the grid labeled "First Reflection."

4. Imagine the figure is reflected again as indicated by Vertical Line 2

5. Sketch the results on the grid labeled "Second Reflection."

6. Still working with Figure 1, tape the pattern blocks together and reflect the figure twice as indicated. Is your sketch the same?

7. Repeat the process with the second figure.

Guided Learning

1. What did you notice when you made the two reflections?

2. What one rotation gives you the same result? *Half-turn*

3. What number of degrees' rotation will produce the same result? *180°*

4. What other reflections are necessary to return the figure to its original position?

Answers

FIRST REFLECTION	SECOND REFLECTION

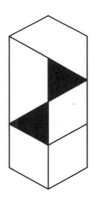	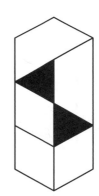

Explore More!

Have the students make a design by coloring pattern block pieces on grid paper. Have them show two lines of reflection. Have them ask a partner to copy their design with pattern blocks and make the reflections about the two lines. Together, they check the partner's work using a mirror.

© Didax – www.didax.com

Double Vision

Name: _____

1. Reflect each figure twice, once about Horizontal Line 1 and then about Vertical Line 2.
2. Record the results of each reflection on the small grids.
3. Check your results with pattern blocks.

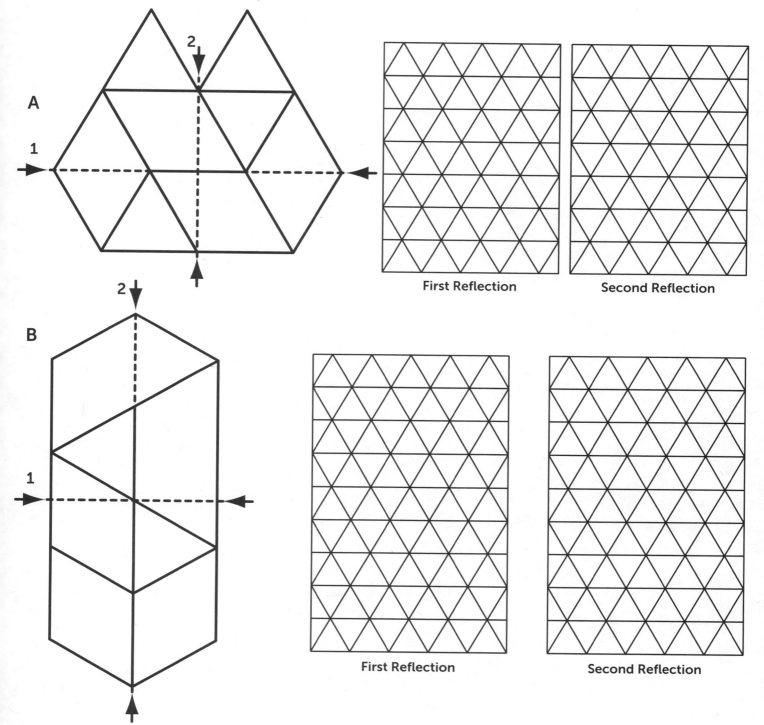

First Reflection

Second Reflection

First Reflection

Second Reflection

Advanced Pattern Block Book

Measurement

Focal Point

Measurement – Develop skills in spatial relationships: arranging, classifying, rotating, and visualizing. Reinforce relationships among area and perimeter.

Materials

- Pattern blocks
  - orange squares only
- Square grid paper (page 135)

Instructions

Have the students make all the different arrangements possible with 5 square pattern blocks (pentominoes), making sure all the squares touch on at least one side. Have them record the different pentominoes on square grid paper. If a pentomino can be flipped and/or turned to fit on another pentomino, it is not considered to be different.

Guided Learning

1. How many different pentominoes did you find?

2. All the pentominoes have the same area (5 square units). Why? Do they all have the same perimeter? Why or why not?

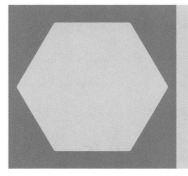

Explore More!

Which pentominoes do you think can fold up to form an open box? Tell the students to put a B on the square that they think would be the bottom of each box. Then, have them cut out the pentominoes and fold them to check their prediction.

Puzzling Pentominoes

Name: _____

Below are all the possible arrangements of orange squares taken two at a time, three at a time, and four at a time. In every arrangement, the squares touch completely along at least one side.

One arrangement of 5 squares is given. Make all the different arrangements possible with 5 squares and record your findings on square grid paper.

1. Dominoes (2 squares)

2. Trominoes (3 squares)

3. Tetrominoes (4 squares)

4. Pentominoes (5 squares)

Focal Point

Measurement – Explore the idea of conservation of area—that is, the area of a figure doesn't change even when its parts are rearranged.

Materials

- Pattern blocks
  - green triangles only

Instructions

Have students use triangles to cover Package A1 and determine its area, using the area of a triangle as one. Then have them rearrange those triangles into a different shape (A2) that will fit on the given grid (A2).

They compare the new area with the original area and sketch the new package on the grid. Have them do the same for Package B1.

Guided Learning

1. Are the areas of the two packages (A1 and A2, B1 and B2) the same? Will this always be true?

2. If the length of one side of a triangle is 1, find the perimeter of the packages. Are the perimeters of each pair the same? Will this always be true?

Double the number of green triangles you just used for Package B1. Make a green package with them.

3. What is the area of the new green package? How does that compare with the area of the original package?

4. What is the new perimeter? How does that compare with the original perimeter?

5. Why does the area of a rearranged package remain the same as the original while the perimeter sometimes changes?

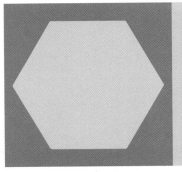

Explore More!

Have the students use triangles to make a package whose perimeter is double that of the original package. What is its area? How does the new area compare to that of the original package. Will this always be true?

© Didax – www.didax.com

Green Packages

Name: _____

1. Assume the area of the green triangle is 1 unit. Cover Package A1 with green triangles. Record the area of the package in the space provided.

2. Rearrange the same triangles on the grid to make a new package (A2). Sketch Package A2 on the grid and record the area.

3. Compare the areas of Packages A1 and A2. Are they the same or different? Explain why.

4. Do the same for Packages B1 and B2.

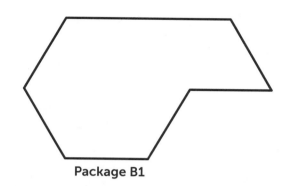

Package A1

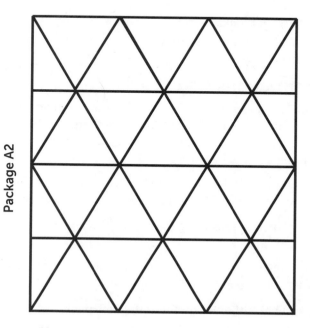

Package A2

A1 area: _____ triangular units

A2 area: _____ triangular units

Are the areas of Packages A1 and A2 the same or different? _____

Why? _____

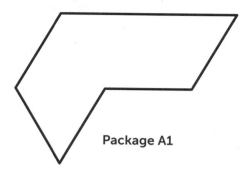

Package B1

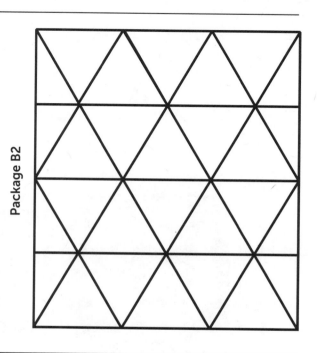

Package B2

B1 area: _____ triangular units

B2 area: _____ triangular units

Are the areas of Packages B1 and B2 the same

or different? _____

Why? _____

Focal Point

Measurement – Explore the relationship between area and perimeter.

Materials

- Pattern Blocks
  - blue rhombuses only

Instructions

Remind the students that blue rhombuses have an area value equal to 2 triangles. Have them use blue rhombuses to make a blue package with an area of 10 triangles.

Ask: If the length of one side of a triangle (and a rhombus) is one, what is the perimeter of your package?

Have the students draw their blue package on the grid labeled A.

Next, have them make a new blue package with an area of 10 but with a different perimeter.

Ask: What is the perimeter of the new package?

Students then draw the package on the grid labeled B.

In the remaining grids, they draw blue packages that match the given information.

Guided Learning

1. Can two figures with the same perimeter have different areas? Give some examples.

2. Can two figures with the same area have different perimeters? Give some examples.

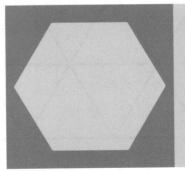

Explore More!

Using blue rhombuses, have the students make a blue package with an area of 8 and a perimeter other than 10. What is the new perimeter? Then, have them make a blue package with a perimeter of 10 and an area other than 8 or 12. What is the area?

© Didax – www.didax.com

Blue Packages

Name: _____

1. Take blue rhombuses and make a blue package with an area of 10. (Remember: 1 blue rhombus has an area equal to 2 triangles.) Draw your blue package on Grid A.

2. Assuming the length of one side of a triangle is 1 unit, find the perimeter of the blue package.

3. Now make another blue package with an area of 10 but with a different perimeter. Draw the package on Grid B.

4. Make and sketch Packages C–F.

Grid A

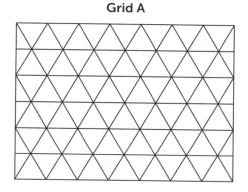

Grid B

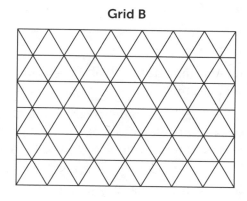

Grid C   Area = 8   Perimeter = 10

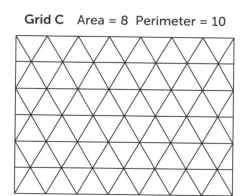

Grid D   Area = 6   Perimeter = 8

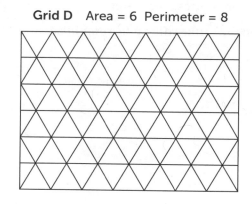

Grid E   Area = 12   Perimeter = 10

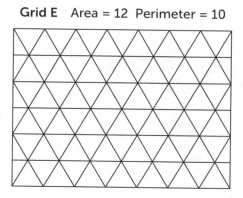

Grid F   Area = 10   Perimeter = 12

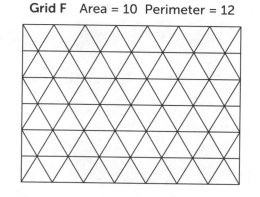

Focal Point

Measurement – Explore the relationship between area and perimeter. Explore how perimeter can vary for figures with fixed areas.

Materials

- Pattern blocks
  - triangles
  - blue rhombuses
  - trapezoids

Instructions

Remind the students that the length of one side of the triangle is equal to 1 unit.

For the first activity, have the students take 6 triangles and make 3 packages of different shapes. In each package, the triangles must touch completely along at least one side.

Have the students sketch the packages, putting "L" on the package with the longest perimeter and "S" on the package with the shortest perimeter.

Have them do the same with 4 blue rhombuses and 4 red trapezoids.

Guided Learning

1. What is the area of each package you sketched?

2. Did the package with the smallest perimeter have the smallest area? Is this always true?

3. Do the packages with the same area always have the same perimeter? Explain. Give an example.

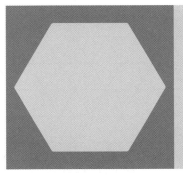

Explore More!

Have the students redo this activity using one of each: triangle, blue rhombus, and trapezoid.

© Didax – www.didax.com

Remodeling

Name: _____

1. Assume the length of one side of a triangle is equal to 1 unit. Take 6 triangles and make 3 different packages. (Remember: the triangles must touch completely on at least one side.)

2. Sketch the packages on the grid. Put "S" on the package with the shortest perimeter and "L" on the package with the longest perimeter. Then fill in the table.

3. Do the same for the blue rhombus and the trapezoid.

Sketch

Shape	Take	Smallest Perimeter	Largest Perimeter
triangle	6	_____ units	_____ units
blue rhombus	4	_____ units	_____ units
trapezoid	4	_____ units	_____ units

Focal Point

Measurement – Identify angles and sides. Determine whether angles are congruent. Reinforce the concept of angles.

Materials

- Pattern blocks
  - One of each

Instructions

Have the students place the corresponding pattern blocks on the outlines A–F. Tell them to trace the edge (or side) of each pattern block with their finger, stopping at the corners. Two edges that have a corner in common form an angle. Have the students record the number of sides, corners, and angles for each pattern block in the space provided on the activity sheet. One angle in each block has been numbered for them.

After the students have determined the number of sides, corners, and angles for each pattern block shape, tell them to look at the mystery shape. Here they will not be able to "feel" the corners. Tell them to use what they have learned to determine the number of sides, corners, and angles in this mystery shape.

Guided Learning

Angles that are the same size are called congruent angles. One way to find out whether angles are congruent is to rotate each pattern block, trying to fit every angle of each block into the corner marked "1." Only the angles that fit exactly into the corner are congruent.

1. Which pattern blocks have all congruent angles?

2. Which pattern blocks have two pairs of congruent angles?

3. Which pattern blocks have no congruent angles? *All have some congruent angles.*

For the Mystery Shape:

4. This shape is made up of several different pattern blocks. Does the number of sides, corners, and angles of the pattern blocks have anything to do with the sides, corners, and angles of the shapes that make up this mystery shape? Why or why not?

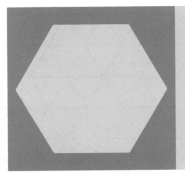

Explore More!

Have the students look at the congruent angles in the hexagon. Does any other pattern block shape have an angle of the same measure? Have them use their pattern blocks to find out which shapes have angles congruent to those in the hexagon.

Name: _____

1. Place the 6 pattern blocks on their corresponding outlines.

2. Trace the edges (perimeter) of each block with your finger, stopping at each corner. Two edges that have a corner in common form an angle.

3. One angle of each block (A–F) has been numbered for you. Fill in the blanks for Blocks A–F and the Mystery Shape.

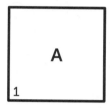

A
1

Number of sides _____
Number of corners _____
Number of angles _____

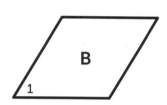

B
1

Number of sides _____
Number of corners _____
Number of angles _____

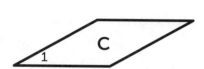

C
1

Number of sides _____
Number of corners _____
Number of angles _____

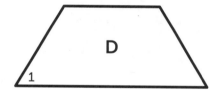

D
1

Number of sides _____
Number of corners _____
Number of angles _____

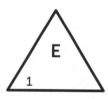

E
1

Number of sides _____
Number of corners _____
Number of angles _____

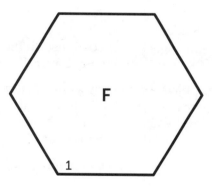

F
1

Number of sides _____
Number of corners _____
Number of angles _____

Mystery Shape

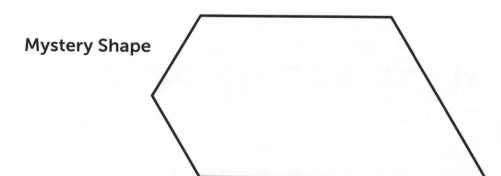

Number of sides _____
Number of corners _____
Number of angles _____

Focal Point

Measurement – Identify angles whose measure is greater than or less than a right angle. Use the words obtuse, acute, and right in relation to angles.

Materials

- Pattern blocks
  - One of each

Instructions

Have the students place the corner of the orange pattern block at the intersection of the two dotted lines on the worksheet. Tell them that these lines intersect to form **right angles**.

Ask: How many right angles does the square contain? Do any of the other pattern blocks have right angles? (On the worksheet, the number of right angles in a square is already filled in.)

Tell students that angles with a measure greater than a right angle are called **obtuse angles**; angles with a measure less than a right angle are called **acute angles**.

Next, have the students compare a right angle in the square pattern block with an angle in the hexagon. They do this by placing one angle over another, making sure one edge of the two pattern blocks is lined up.

Ask: Is Angle 1 on the hexagon greater than a right angle or smaller?
It is greater.

Have the students look next at Angle 2 and so on. In the space next to the hexagon, they describe the angles they found.

Students then investigate the angles of the other pattern blocks and record their answers on the worksheet.

Guided Learning

1. How many shapes have right angles? Acute angles? Obtuse angles?

2. Can a shape have both acute angles and obtuse angles? Explain.

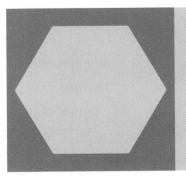

Explore More!

Using 1, 2, 3, or 4 pattern blocks, can you construct or identify a figure with fewer than 3 angles? Why or why not?

© Didax – www.didax.com

Blocks, Corners, and Intersections

Name: _____

The two dotted lines below intersect to form right angles. Place the corner of the orange pattern block at the intersection of the two lines and note that the corner forms a right angle. How many right angles does the square have?

Compare the angles of the pattern blocks listed below to the right angle of the orange square. Are the angles bigger or smaller? Do any of the other pattern blocks have right angles?

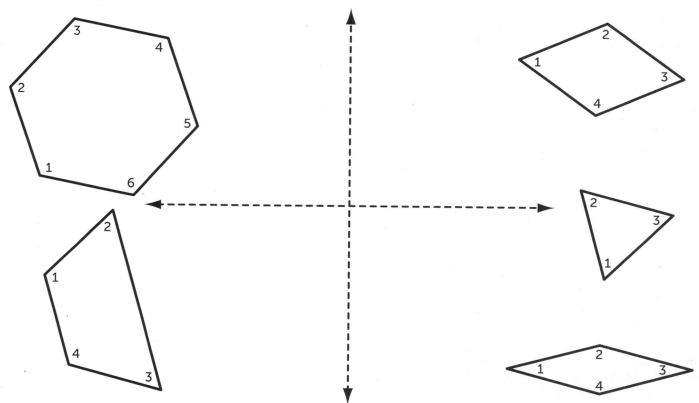

Below, describe the angles you investigated in each figure.

1. SQUARE: _____ All 4 angles are right angles. _____

2. HEXAGON: _____

3. TRAPEZOID: _____

4. BLUE RHOMBUS: _____

5. TRIANGLE: _____

6. TAN RHOMBUS: _____

Focal Point

Measurement – Identify obtuse, acute, right, straight, and reflex angles.

Materials

- Pattern blocks

Instructions

Guide students through the two activities on the worksheet as follows:

Activity 1:

Two right angles sharing a common corner form a **straight angle**. You can also form a straight angle by placing two or more pattern blocks together to form a straight line.

Sketch three different ways of forming a straight angle on the lines given. Note that two angles that form a straight angle are called **supplementary angles**.

Activity 2:

Most of the angles we have been looking at have a measure of less than 180 degrees. But many geometric figures also have **reflex angles**, angles whose measure is greater than 180 degrees. One reflex angle in each figure is marked with an "X"; look at them now.

For this exercise, you will identify all the angles inside the figures. Mark angles as right (R), acute (A), obtuse (O), or reflex (X). Write your answers next to each angle on your worksheet.

Guided Learning

1. How does an acute angle compare to a right angle?

2. How does an obtuse angle compare to a right angle?

3. How does a straight angle compare to a right angle?

4. Order these types of angles from greatest to smallest: acute, obtuse, straight, right.

5. What are supplementary angles?

6. Which pattern blocks have both acute and obtuse angles?

7. Which pattern blocks have only acute angles? Only right angles? Only obtuse angles?

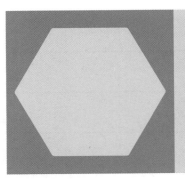

Explore More!

Tell the students that a right angle can also be formed by putting together two blocks to form an angle that has the same measure as an angle on an orange square. Can they find two different ways to do that? Two angles that form a right angle are called **complementary angles.**

Name: _____

ACTIVITY 1

Two right angles sharing a common corner form a **straight angle**.

Straight angles can also be formed by placing the corners of two or more blocks together. Two examples are shown. Find at least three more ways to make a straight angle using two or more pattern blocks.

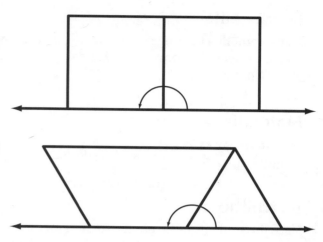

Name other pairs of blocks that can form straight angles:

1. _____   2. _____   3. _____

ACTIVITY 2

You have just been learning about **right, acute, obtuse,** and straight angles. Some angles are greater than straight angles; these are called **reflex angles**.

For each figure below, first put an X on each reflex angle (one reflex angle in each figure has already been marked). Then put an R on each right angle, an A on each acute angle, and an O on each obtuse angle.

A.

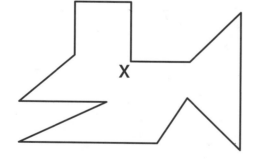

B.

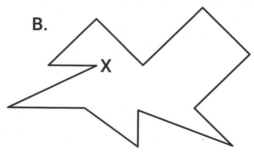

C.

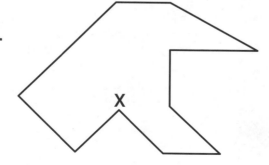

Focal Point

Measurement – Investigate straight angles using symmetry. Develop the concept of a fixed size for angles about a point.

Materials

- Pattern blocks
- Rulers

Instructions

Have the students place orange squares on the flower on the left side of the worksheet. Then have them place blue rhombuses on the flower on the right.

Say: Flowers can be formed by making straight angles above and below a horizontal straight line. Now make a one-color flower using green triangles. Construct half of the flower above the straight line provided. Then construct its reflection below the line. Ask: How many green triangles do you need to make the flower?

Using the tan rhombus, students make a one-color flower above and below the straight line.

Students choose other blocks to make two-color and three-color flowers above and below a horizontal line. Have them record their work on the back of the activity page or on a separate sheet of paper.

Guided Learning

1. How many orange squares were needed to make the straight angle?

   2

   Since a right angle is 90 degrees, what is the measure of the straight angle?

   180 degrees

2. How many acute angles of the blue rhombus were needed to form the straight angle?

   3

   How many degrees are in each acute angle of the blue rhombus?

   60

3. How many acute angles of the tan rhombus were needed to form the straight angle?

   6

   How many degrees are in each acute angle of the tan rhombus?

   30

4. Place your finger on the center of each flower. How many degrees are needed to complete each flower (around the center)?

   360 degrees

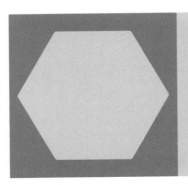

Explore More!

Using the method described above, have the students try to make a flower with petals of 4 and then 5 colors. Is this possible? Why or why not? Have them use what they know about right, acute, and obtuse angles to answer this question.

© Didax – www.didax.com

Forming Flowers

Name: _____

Flowers of one color can be formed by making straight angles above and below a straight line.

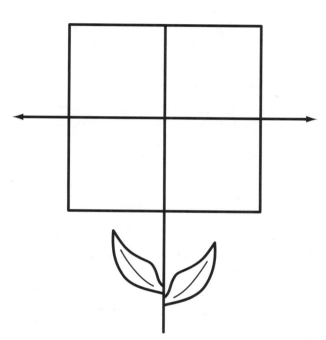

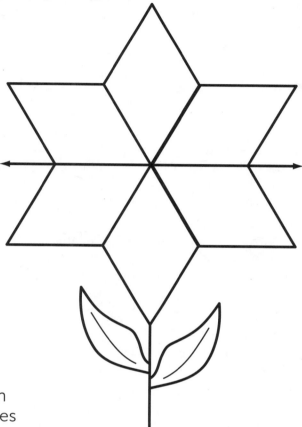

1. Place one acute angle of the tan rhombus on the line at the right. How many tan rhombuses do you think you need to make a one-color flower? _____

2. Complete the top half of the tan flower and then make its reflection. How many tan rhombuses did you need? _____

3. As the angle at the center of the one-color flowers get smaller, do you need more blocks or fewer blocks to make the flower?

   _____

4. On a separate sheet of paper, draw a horizontal line with your ruler and make an original two-color flower. Remove the blocks and sketch your flower.

5. Make an original three-color flower. Sketch it.

© Didax – www.didax.com

Focal Point

Measurement – Introduce the concept of degrees in angle measurement.

Materials

• Pattern blocks

Instructions

Remind students that in the Forming Flowers activity, they put together pattern blocks to form a straight angle above and below a horizontal straight line. The two straight angles also formed the central angle of the flower—a circle, which equals 360 degrees.

Have the students place orange squares on the figure at the top right side of the worksheet. Ask: How many orange squares does it take to fill the space around the central point shown by the arrow on the figure? *4*

Say: The angle around that point is 360 degrees. So, each angle of the 4 orange squares that cover that point should be 360 divided by 4, or 90 degrees. We can use this measure of 90 degrees to help us find out the measure of all the angles of our pattern blocks.

Have the students place the tan rhombus next. Ask: How many acute angles of the tan rhombus does it take to exactly cover a right angle? *3*

How many degrees are in one acute angle of a tan rhombus? *30, or 90 divided by 3*

Have the students find the measure of the angles indicated and record their answers in the spaces provided. They may use pattern blocks to help, if necessary.

Guided Learning

1. How many right angles form the central angle of the circle? *4*

2. What is the measure of the central angle? *360 degrees* The right angle? *90 degrees*

3. What is the measure of the obtuse angles of the blue rhombus and the hexagon? *120 degrees*

4. What is the measure of the obtuse angles of the tan rhombus? *150 degrees*

5. What is the measure of the acute angles of the triangle and the blue rhombus? *60 degrees*

6. What is the measure of the acute angles of the tan rhombus? *30 degrees*

7. Which angles of the pattern blocks are complementary? Explain.

8. Which angles of the pattern blocks are supplementary? Explain.

Explore More!

Have the students find the measure of a straight angle and justify their answer.

© Didax – www.didax.com

Degree Power

Name: _____

As you will recall from the Forming Flowers activity (page 83), a circle is the geometric figure that all one-color "flowers" have in common. The central angle of the circle measures 360 degrees.

Put 4 orange squares on the circle to the right.

1. The central angle of any circle contains 4 right angles. How many degrees are in each right angle? _____

2. Since 3 acute angles of the tan rhombus make a right angle, how many degrees are in each acute angle?_____
How do you know?_____
_____
_____

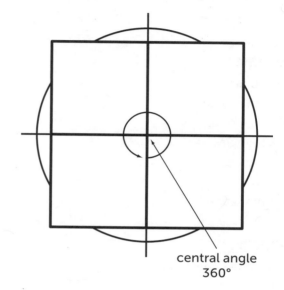

central angle
360°

Using the acute angle of the tan rhombus, find the measure of each of the following angles.

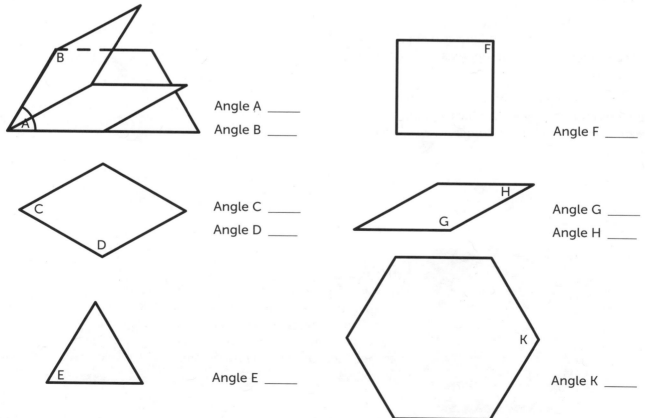

Angle A _____
Angle B _____

Angle F _____

Angle C _____
Angle D _____

Angle G _____
Angle H _____

Angle E _____

Angle K _____

Focal Point

Measurement – Reinforce the concept of measurement of angles to determine that (a) the sum of the angles of a triangle equals 180 degrees and (b) the sum of the angles of a quadrilateral equals 360 degrees.

Materials

- Pattern blocks
  - 3 tan rhombuses
  - 1 blue rhombus
  - 6 triangles
  - 2 trapezoids
  - 1 square
  - 1 hexagon

Instructions

Reinforce the understanding that the number of degrees in a circle, the measure of the central angle, is 360 degrees. Remind students that since 4 right angles cover the central angle, the measure of each right angle is 90 degrees.

Ask: What is the measure of the acute angle of the tan rhombus? *30 degrees* Have the students explain their answer. *3 acute angles of the tan rhombus are congruent to the right angle.*

Have the students use pattern blocks to find the angle measurements of the triangle, the blue rhombus, and the trapezoid, and record their findings in the spaces provided.

Guided Learning

1. What is the sum of the measure of the angles in a triangle? Explain.

2. What is the sum of the measure of the angles in a square? Explain.

3. What is the sum of the measure of the angles in a blue rhombus? Explain.

4. Using what you have learned, what would you predict to be the sum of the measure of the angles in the tan rhombus? Explain.

5. Is the sum of the measure of the angles of the trapezoid 540 degrees? Why not? How many sides does the trapezoid have? Angles? Where did Pedro make an error?

6. What is the sum of the measure of all of the angles of a quadrilateral? Why?

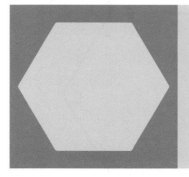

Explore More!

The yellow hexagon equals 2 trapezoids or 6 triangles. Have the students predict the sum of the measure of its angles. Using what they have learned about measurement, have them find the measure of each angle of the hexagon. Then, have them find the sum of the measure of its angles.

 © Didax – www.didax.com

Sum Angles

Name: _____

The right angle (90°) of the square can be formed by putting together the acute angles of 3 tan rhombuses. Therefore, the measure of each acute angle of a tan rhombus is 30°.

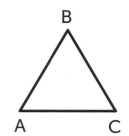

Find the measure of each angle of triangle ABC.

Angle A = _____
Angle B = _____
Angle C= _____

The sum of the measure of the angles of the triangle is _____.

James says, "The blue rhombus is equivalent to two triangles. Therefore, the measure of its angles is 360 degrees."

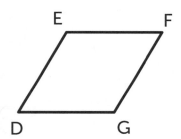

Find the measure of each angle of the blue rhombus DEFG.

Angle D = _____
Angle E = _____
Angle F = _____
Angle G = _____

The sum of the measure of the angles of the blue rhombus is

_____.

Pedro says, "The trapezoid is equivalent to the blue rhombus and the triangle. Therefore, the measure of its angles is 360 degrees plus 180 degrees, or 540 degrees total."

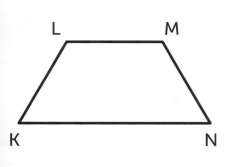

Find the measure of each angle of trapezoid KLMN.

Angle K = _____
Angle L = _____
Angle M = _____
Angle N = _____

Is the sum 540°? Explain. _____

Find the sum of the measure of the angles of the tan rhombus and the square. Is the sum of the measure of the angles the same for all pattern block quadrilaterals? _____

_____

5

Advanced Pattern Block Book

Algebra

Algebra: **Building Patterns**

Focal Point

Algebra/Reasoning and Proof – Use, represent, and extend patterns. Make and evaluate conjectures using a variety of strategies.

Materials

- Pattern blocks

Instructions

Have the students do the following:

1. For Exercises 1–3, construct the first three terms of the pattern pictures with pattern blocks.

2. Examine how the pattern changes from Term 1 to Term 3.

3. Decide how the pattern will grow in Terms 4 and 5.

4. Use pattern blocks to extend the pattern.

5. Extend the remaining patterns to Term 5.

6. Sketch Terms 4 and 5 for each pattern.

Guided Learning

1. How does each pattern change from term to term?

2. Do you need more pattern blocks to create the terms?

3. Is the pattern increasing or decreasing in some way?

4. Is it a repeating pattern?

Explore More!

Have the students look at this pattern:

Each one of the choices below could complete the pattern. Explain why each is possible. Can they think of another choice?

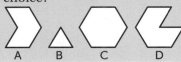

© Didax – www.didax.com

Name: _____

Make each of the following patterns with pattern blocks. Then decide what comes next. Record your solutions. Since there is often more than one possibility, be ready to explain your choice.

1.

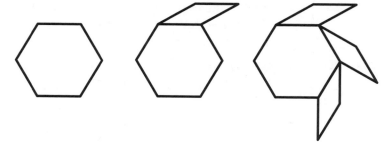

_____

2.

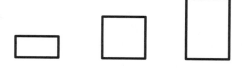

_____

3.

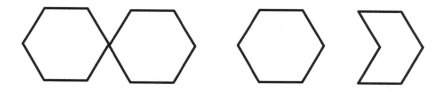

_____

4.

_____

5.

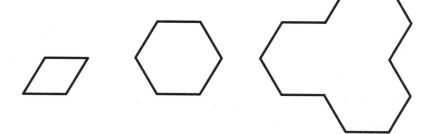

_____

6.

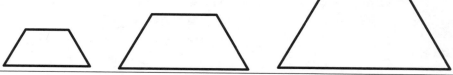

_____

Focal Point

Algebra/Problem Solving – Create and explain patterns using concrete objects. Analyze problems by observing patterns.

Materials

- Pattern blocks

Instructions

Have the students do the following:

1. Use pattern block triangles to create Terms A, B, and C of the pattern illustrated on the worksheet. Note that the shaded triangles are empty spaces.

2. Count the number of green triangles used in each term and record them in the space provided for A, B, and C.

3. Analyze how the terms are changing (growing).

4. Build Triangle D.

5. Complete the table for D, E, and F.

Guided Learning

1. What pattern do you see?

2. How are the terms changing?

3. What is the total number of triangles used at each term through F.
   1, 3, 6, 10, 15, 21

4. Why do you think these numbers are called triangular numbers?

Explore More!

Have the students make the same triangular patterns, but this time tell them not to leave any spaces between the green triangles. For example, the first triangle will use 1 green triangle, the second triangle will use 4, and the third will use 9. Have them make a table like the one shown and fill in their table for at least 6 "filled" triangles. What is the number sequence now?

Name: _____

Make triangles of different sizes, as shown below.
(The shaded triangles are empty spaces.)

C.

B.

A.

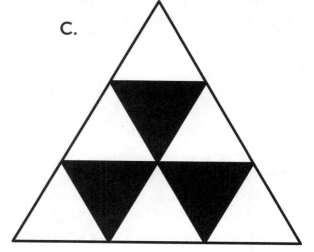

1. Count the number of green triangles needed for each one. How many green triangles are needed to build Triangle D (the next larger similar triangle)? Record.

A = _____   B = _____   C = _____   D = _____

2. For each successive triangle formed, a new base can be added, increasing the length by one. Using this pattern, how many green triangles would you need to make Triangles E and F (the next larger similar triangles)?

E = _____   F = _____

3. Complete the table.

Triangle	Number of Green Triangles	Total Number of Green Triangles
A	1	1
B	1 + 2	3
C	1 + 2 + 3	6
D		
E		
F		

4. The numbers in the sequence are 1, 3, 6, _____, _____, _____.

Algebra: **Square Numbers**

Focal Point

Algebra/Problem Solving – Analyze problems by observing patterns. Create algebraic or geometric patterns using concrete objects or visual drawings.

Materials

- Pattern blocks

Instructions

Have the students do the following:

1. Use pattern block squares to create Terms A, B, and C of the pattern illustrated on the worksheet.

2. Count the number of squares needed for each one.

3. Decide how the pattern will grow in Term D, and decide how many orange squares they will need to build it.

4. Record how many squares were needed for Terms A–D in the spaces provided.

5. Explain in writing how the pattern is growing.

6. Ask themselves how many squares are needed for Terms E and F.

7. Complete the table and the number sequence.

Guided Learning

1. What patterns do you see?

2. Describe the changes in the squares from Term A through Term F.

3. The total number of squares in Terms A–D form the sequence 1, 4, 9, 16, ... What are the next 3 numbers in the sequence?
   25, 36, 49

4. Why do you think these numbers are called square numbers?

Explore More!

How many odd numbers are added to get the fourth square number? The fifth? The ninth? The tenth?

What is the sum of the first 50 odd numbers? *2,500*

Which square number is this? *fiftieth*

   © Didax – www.didax.com

Square Numbers

Name: _____

Make squares of increasing size, as shown below, using your pattern blocks.

C.

B.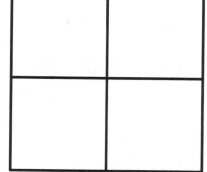

A.

1. Count the number of orange squares needed for each one. How many orange squares are needed to build Square D (the square that is next in size)?

   A = _____   B = _____   C = _____   D = _____

2. How is the pattern growing? _____

   _____

   _____

3. How many orange squares are needed for Squares E and F?

   E = _____   F = _____

4. Complete the table.

Square	Number of Orange Squares	Total Number of Orange Squares
A	1	1
B	1 + 3	4
C	1 + 3 + 5	9
D		
E		
F		

5. Complete the number sequence: 1, 4, 9, _____, _____, _____

Focal Point

Algebra/Problem Solving – Analyze problems by observing patterns. Create and explain patterns and algebraic relationships.

Materials

- Pattern blocks
- Triangular grid paper (page 136)

Instructions

Have the students do the following:

1. Take the tan rhombus. Build the next similar shape with the pattern blocks and record how many blocks were needed in the space provided. *4*

2. Build the next two similar shapes, recording the number of blocks needed.

3. Do the same thing for the blue rhombus and the trapezoid.

4. Complete the tables and look for a pattern to determine how many blocks are needed for the fifth and sixth similar shapes.

Note: When making similar trapezoids, students must rearrange the red pattern blocks to make the next term. They cannot just add a row of blocks.

Guided Learning

1. How did the tan rhombus pattern grow from Term 1 to Term 4? the blue rhombus? the trapezoid?

2. What number pattern do you have for each shape?

3. Do any of the shapes have the same number pattern? Why?

4. Do the number of pattern blocks used produce a sequence of triangular or square numbers? Why?

Explore More!

Building rectangles produces a sequence of rectangular numbers. Have the students use orange squares to build rectangles A and B. Then have them build the next two rectangles in the pattern.

Have the students complete the table and predict the seventh rectangular number in this sequence. Tell them to look for a pattern that will help them predict any number in the sequence.

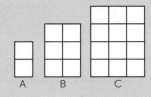

Rectangle	Dimensions	Total Number of Orange Squares
A	2 x 1	2
B	3 x 2	6
C		
D		
E		
F		

Triangular or Square Numbers

Name: _____

Build shapes of increasing size that are similar to each of the pattern blocks shown below.

1. How many blocks would you use each time if you built the second, third, and fourth bigger shapes? Record below.

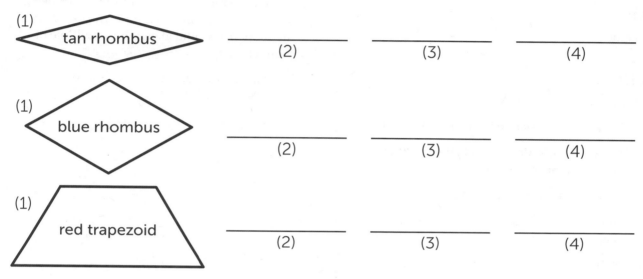

(1) tan rhombus _____ (2) _____ (3) _____ (4)

(1) blue rhombus _____ (2) _____ (3) _____ (4)

(1) red trapezoid _____ (2) _____ (3) _____ (4)

2. Complete the tables below. Look for a pattern. How many blocks would you need to build the fifth and sixth bigger shapes that are also similar?

Shape ◇	Number of Blocks
1	1
2	4
3	
4	
5	
6	

Shape ◇	Number of Blocks
1	
2	
3	
4	
5	
6	

Shape ▱	Number of Blocks
1	
2	
3	
4	
5	
6	

3. Use triangular grid paper to illustrate how you would form the second, third, and fourth shapes for the trapezoid.

Focal Point

Algebra/Problem Solving – Make organized lists to solve numerical problems. Create and explain patterns and algebraic relationships.

Materials

- Pattern blocks

Instructions

Have the students do the following:

1. Cover Diagram A in the worksheet with triangles.

2. Cover Diagram B with triangles. Ask themselves: How many do you need?

3. Record their findings on the given table.

4. Find out how many triangles they need to cover 3, 4, and 5 hexagons.

5. Complete the table.

6. Look at the pattern in the table and answer questions 2, 3, and 4.

7. Explain in writing how they would find the number of triangles for *n* hexagons.

8. Write the rule in the space provided.

Guided Learning

1. How does the number of triangles change as you increase the number of hexagons? Why?

2. The numbers in the numerical sequence will always be a multiple of which number? Why?

3. If you were increasing the number of trapezoids instead of hexagons each time, the numbers in the sequence would always be a multiple of which number? Why?

4. What is the rule for finding the number of triangles for *n* trapezoids? *n x 3*

Explore More!

Using only triangles, have the students make the apple shown. How many triangles do they need? Have them make a table showing how many triangles are needed to make 1 apple, 2 apples, 3 apples, ... 10 apples. Have them predict how many triangles are needed to make 100 apples, 199 apples. Why do they think so?

Numer of Apples	Number of Triangles
1	7
2	14
3	21
10	70
100	700
199	1,393

© Didax – www.didax.com

Hexagons or Triangles

Name: _____

Six triangles make a hexagon. How many triangles do you need to make 2 hexagons? Cover the 2 hexagons below.

1. How many triangles do you need to make 3 hexagons? 5 hexagons? Complete the table below.

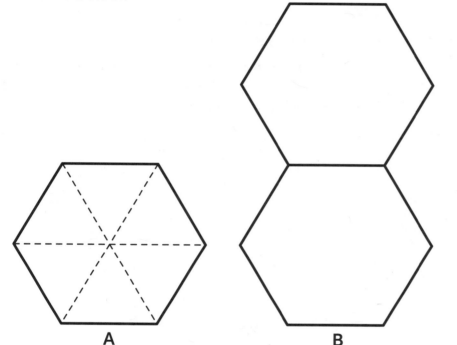

A   B

Number of Hexagons	Number of Triangles
1	6
2	
3	
4	
5	
6	
7	
8	
9	
10	

Look at the pattern in the table.

2. How many triangles would you need to make 50 hexagons? _____ triangles

3. How many triangles would you need to make 100 hexagons? _____ triangles

4. How many triangles would you need to make 199 hexagons? _____ triangles

5. Explain in writing how you would find the number of triangles for any number (*n*) of hexagons. _____

_____

_____

_____

6. Write a rule for finding the number of triangles for any number (*n*) of hexagons.

_____

Algebra: **Creating Stars**

Focal Point

Algebra/Problem Solving – Make organized lists to solve numerical patterns. Write an equation to represent a function from a table of values.

Materials

• Pattern blocks

Instructions

Have the students do the following:

1. Use blue rhombuses to create a star like the one shown on the worksheet.

2. Place triangles on top of the blue rhombus star.

3. Write the number of triangles needed to make a congruent star in the space provided in the table.

4. Build another star that is congruent to the first star. How many blue rhombuses do they need to make 2 stars? How many triangles? Record their answers in the table.

5. Build 3, 4, and 5 stars. Look for the numerical pattern.

6. Complete the table through 10 stars without making additional pattern block stars.

7. Answer questions 1 through 6.

8. Write a rule for finding the number of triangles for any number (*n*) of stars.

Guided Learning

1. Look at the stars formed by blue rhombuses in the table. The number of blue rhombuses (4, 8, 12, ...) is always a multiple of 4. Why?

2. The number of triangles is always a multiple of what number? Why?

3. What is the relationship of the number of blue rhombuses to triangles? *1 to 2*

4. What is the relationship for the number of stars to blue rhombuses? *1 to 4*

5. What is the relationship for the number of stars to triangles? *1 to 8*

6. What is the algebraic equation for finding the number of triangles "*T*" for any number of stars "*n*"? *n = 8T*

Explore More!

Have the students make a bridge, as shown. How many trapezoids did they use? How many triangles could form a congruent figure?

Have them make a table indicating how many trapezoids and how many triangles are needed to make 1 bridge, 2 bridges, 3 bridges, ... , 10 bridges; to make 1,000 bridges; to make 999 bridges.

Numer of Bridges	Number of Trapezoids	Number of Triangles
1	3	9
2	6	18
3	9	27
10	30	90
1,000	3,000	9,000

© Didax – www.didax.com

Creating Stars

Name: _____

Using blue rhombuses, Elizabeth formed a star like the one shown. Cover the blue rhombus star with triangles.

Number of Stars	Number of Blue Rhombuses	Number of Triangles
1		
2		
3		
4		
5		
6		
7		
8		
9		
10		

Record all your answers to questions 1–3 in the table. Then look at the pattern in the table and answer questions 4–7.

1. How many triangles did you need to make a congruent star? _____

2. How many blue rhombuses would you need to make 2 stars? _____ 5 stars? _____

3. How many triangles would you need to make 2 congruent stars? _____ 5 stars? _____

4. How many blue rhombuses would you need to make 50 stars? _____ 49 stars? _____ 200 stars? _____

5. How many triangles would you need to make 50 stars? _____ 49 stars? _____ 200 stars? _____

6. Explain in writing how you would find the number of blue rhombuses for any number (n) of stars. _____

   _____

   _____

7. Write a rule for finding the number of triangles for any number (n) of stars.

   _____

Algebra: **Discovering Formulas**

Focal Point

Algebra/Geometry – Evaluate formulas for area for given input values. Determine the area of rectangles and develop formulas.

Materials

- Pattern blocks
- Square grid paper (page 135)

Instructions

Have the students do the following:

1. Take pattern block squares and cover the figure (rectangle #1). Record its length and width in the space provided.

2. Take the same number of squares and make another rectangle (rectangle #2). Record its length and width in the space provided.

3. If possible, make another rectangle with the same number of squares.

4. Record all the information in the table.

5. Build rectangles using 18 square pattern blocks and record their findings in the table.

6. Make a rectangle with a length of 8 squares and a width of 3 squares. How many orange squares do they need to cover this rectangle?
   Area = 24 squares
   Make as many rectangles as possible with 24 squares and record their findings in the table.

Guided Learning

1. What do we mean by the word *area*?

2. Using 24 squares, how many different rectangles did you make?

3. What remained the same about all the rectangles you made with 24 squares?

4. What changed?

5. How can you find the area of a rectangle when you know its length and width?

6. What is the formula for finding the area *(A)* of any rectangle when you know its length *(l)* and width *(w)*?

Explore More!

Have the students predict the dimensions of all possible rectangles with an area of 36 square units. Have them outline the rectangles on square grid paper, where possible, and record the dimensions. For each new 36-square-unit rectangle they form, what remains the same and what changes? Have them check the area of each rectangle using the formula for area.

 © Didax – www.didax.com

Discovering Formulas

Name: _____

Cover the rectangle with orange squares.

1. If the orange square has an area of 1 square unit, what is the area of the figure? _____ square units

2. How many squares wide is it? _____

3. How many squares long is it? _____

Take the squares you used to cover this figure and rearrange them to make another rectangular figure.

4. What is the area of the new figure? _____ square units

5. What is its width? _____

6. What is its length? _____

Record the dimensions of the two rectangles in the table below. Rearrange the blocks again.

7. Using 12 squares, can you form a third rectangular figure whose dimensions are different from the first two? Record the dimensions in the table below.

8. Now use 18 blocks to build all the rectangles possible. What size rectangles can you form? Record the dimensions in the table below.

Total Area	Rectangle 1		Rectangle 2		Rectangle 3		Rectangle 4	
	Width	Length	Width	Length	Width	Length	Width	Length
12								
18								
24								

9. Make a rectangle with a length of 8 and a width of 3. What is its area? _____ How many squares did you use? _____

Continue rearranging the 24 blocks until you have made all the rectangles possible. Record the area, length, and width of each arrangement in the table.

10. Explain how you would find the area of a rectangle when you know its length and width. _____

_____

11. Write a formula that will give the area (A) of any rectangle when you know its length (l) and width (w). _____

Focal Point

Algebra/Problem Solving – Model problems with pictures/diagrams or physical objects. Introduce algebraic procedures to solve simple one-step equations.

Materials

- Pattern blocks

Instructions

Have the students look at the example. Tell them that a bag containing 1 "secret" pattern block was placed on the left side of a balance. On the right side, 3 triangles were placed. The triangles are equivalent in area to the pattern block in the bag.

Have them use the triangles shown on the right side of the balance to identify the secret pattern block that has the same area. In the example, the secret block is a trapezoid. To complete the exercise, the students write the name of the block in the space provided.

Have the students follow the same procedure for Exercises 1–3. The number on the bag tells how many of the same block are hidden inside.

For Exercises 4–8, there are extra triangles next to the bag with the secret block(s). To solve the problems, the students must remove the extra triangles so that the bag is by itself on the left side of the balance. They must also remove the same number of triangles on the right side to keep the scales balanced and to determine what is in the bag.

Guided Learning

1. Which one pattern block covers the same area as 2 triangles? 3 triangles? 6 triangles?

2. Which one pattern block would balance a scale with 3 blue rhombuses on the right side?

3. In Exercises 4–8, why must you remove the same number of triangles from each side of the balance to find the secret block?

Note: For these problems, we are assuming that the bag itself has no (or negligible) weight.

Explore More!

Have the students write two balance problems to uncover the secret block(s). This time the right side of the balance has any number of blue rhombuses instead of triangles. Have them decide what should be in the bag on the left side and explain why.

Balances

Name: _____

(Uncover the Secret Block)

Example: On the left side of the balance is a bag with a pattern block hidden inside. On the right side are 3 triangles. Which one block has the same area as 3 triangles? Use your pattern blocks to find out.

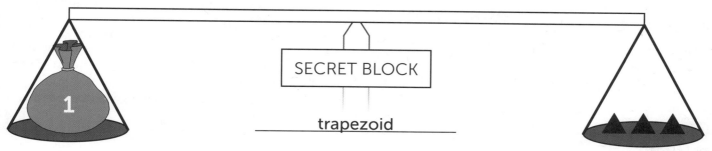

_____ trapezoid

The bag on the left side of the balance tells the number of pattern blocks hidden inside. The triangles on the right side of the balance are equal in area to the secret block(s). Use your pattern blocks to identify the secret block(s). Write the answer in the space provided.

1. _____

2. _____

3. _____

Note: The scale must always be balanced. If you remove a block from one side to help uncover the secret block(s), you must remove the same block from the other side.

Find more secret blocks.

4. _____

5. _____

6. _____

7. _____

8. _____

Algebra: **Grab Bag Mystery**

Focal Point

Algebra/Problem Solving – Understand that numerical information can be represented arithmetically and algebraically. Use guess and check to solve problems. Use a table to create algebraic patterns and organize data.

Materials

- Pattern blocks
  - triangles
  - blue rhombuses
  - trapezoids

Instructions

Have the students read through the problem at the top of the activity page. Remind them that 1 blue rhombus is equivalent to 2 triangles and 1 trapezoid is equivalent to 3 triangles.

Then, have the students solve the mystery using pattern blocks and the table provided to "guess and check" their answers.

Tell them to look at the first guess. If Dana picked 10 blue rhombuses and no trapezoids, she would have 20 triangles. 27 triangles are needed to solve the mystery.

Next, have them try 9 rhombuses + 1 trapezoid (10 blocks). 9 rhombuses = 18 triangles and 1 trapezoid = 3 triangles. 18 + 3 = 21 triangles.

Have the students look for a pattern and complete the table to find 10 blocks equaling 27 triangles.

Guided Learning

1. Look at the table. Which 10 pieces could Dana have taken if they were exchanged for 25 triangles? Why? *5 rhombuses + 5 trapezoids = 10 triangles + 15 triangles = 25*

2. Look at the table. What happens every time you exchange a rhombus for a trapezoid to still have 10 blocks? Explain.

3. If Dana started by taking 10 trapezoids and no rhombuses, how many triangles could they be exchanged for? *30 triangles*
   Since that is too many triangles, what would you do?

Explore More!

Say to the students: Suppose you put your hand in the bag and this time you grabbed 20 pieces that could be exchanged for 51 triangles. How many blue rhombuses and how many trapezoids would you have taken?

                    © Didax – www.didax.com

Grab Bag Mystery

Name: _____

Without looking, Dana puts her hand into a bag of pattern blocks containing only blue rhombuses and trapezoids and pulls some out. Her friend tells her that she took 10 blocks, and if each block is exchanged for the correct number of triangles, she will have 27 triangles.

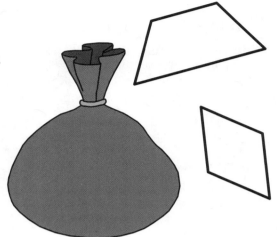

How many rhombuses and how many trapezoids did Dana take? Try to solve the mystery using the pattern blocks.

Use the table to help solve the mystery.

Number of Blue Rhombuses	Number of Trapezoids	Number of △ Replacing the Blue Rhombuses	Number of △ Replacing the Trapezoids	Total Number of Triangles
10	0	20	0	20
9	1	18	3	21
8	2		6	

1. If Dana picked 10 blue rhombuses and no trapezoids, she would have 20 triangles. If she picked 9 blue rhombuses and 1 trapezoid, she would have _____ triangles.

Continue trying out the different possibilities using the table.

2. How many of each kind would Dana have taken if all 10 blocks could be exchanged for 25 triangles? _____

_____

Algebra: **More Grab Bag Fun**

Focal Point

Algebra/Problem Solving – Understand that numerical information can be represented arithmetically and algebraically. Use guess and check to solve problems. Use a table to create algebraic patterns and organize data.

Materials

- Pattern blocks
  - trapezoids
  - hexagons
  - triangles

Instructions

Have the students read through the problem at the top of the activity page. Remind them that 1 hexagon is equivalent to 6 triangles and 1 trapezoid is equivalent to 3 triangles. Then, with a partner, have them solve the problem using pattern blocks and the table provided.

This time, instead of guessing that all 17 blocks are trapezoids and there are no hexagons (which would be equivalent to 51 triangles), have them guess using about the same number of trapezoids and hexagons. (Example: 9 hexagons and 8 trapezoids are equivalent to 78 triangles.) Ask: Why is this a good strategy?

Have the students make the necessary exchanges to get 17 blocks that are equivalent to 87 triangles.

Guided Learning

1. The first guess in the table is 9 hexagons and 8 trapezoids, which are exchanged for 78 triangles. To get more triangles, do you increase the hexagons so that you have 10 hexagons and 7 trapezoids, or do you increase the trapezoids so that you have 8 hexagons and 9 trapezoids? Why?
   Increase the hexagons. Increasing the trapezoids actually decreases the number of triangles.

2. What happens every time you exchange one hexagon for a trapezoid so that you still have 17 blocks? Why?
   The number of triangles goes up by 3 because hexagons are worth 6 triangles, while trapezoids are worth only 3 triangles.

3. If 6 times the number of hexagons *(H)* gives you the number *(n)* of triangles, and 3 times the number of trapezoids *(T)* gives you the number *(n)* of triangles, what number sentence shows the total number of triangles? $n = 6H + 3T$
   What number sentence shows the number of hexagons (H) plus the number of trapezoids *(T)* equals 17? $H + T = 17$

Explore More!

Say to the students: Suppose you put your hand into the bag, and this time you grab fewer than 20 pieces. Your partner tells you that you have picked the same number of hexagons and trapezoids and that they can be exchanged for 45 triangles. How many of each kind of block did you pick? Tell them to use the table to help find the answer.

Number of Hexagons	Number of Trapezoids	Number of △ Replacing the Hexagons	Number of △ Replacing the Trapezoids	Total Number of Triangles
1	1	6	3	9
2	2	12	6	18

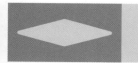

More Grab Bag Fun

Name: _____

Without looking, Mary Grace puts her hand into a bag of pattern blocks containing only trapezoids and hexagons and pulls some out. Her friend tells her that she took 17 blocks, and if each block is exchanged for the correct number of triangles, she will have 87 triangles.

How many trapezoids and how many hexagons did Mary Grace take?

Use the table to help solve the mystery.

Number of Hexagons	Number of Trapezoids	Number of △ Replacing the Hexagons	Number of △ Replacing the Trapezoids	Total Number of Triangles
9	8	54	24	78
10	7	60	21	81

1. If she took an almost equal number of trapezoids and hexagons, Mary Grace could have pulled out 9 hexagons and 8 trapezoids (17 blocks). What would happen if she increased the number of hexagons? Why? _____

_____

2. If 6 times the number of hexagons (*H*) gives you the number (*n*) of triangles, and 3 times the number of trapezoids (*T*) gives you the number (*n*) of triangles, write a sentence that shows the total number (*n*) of triangles for the hexagons (*H*) and trapezoids (*T*). _____

3. Write another sentence that shows that the number of hexagons and the number of trapezoids equal 17. _____

Advanced Pattern Block Book

Probability & Statistics

Focal Point

Statistics and Probability – Collect, organize, display, and analyze data. Represent data using bar graphs.

Materials

- Pattern blocks
- Square grid paper

Instructions

Have the students do the following:

1. Cover the grid on activity page 1, using pattern blocks to make an original design. For example, they may decide to cover 6 triangles with a hexagon, with 2 trapezoids or 3 rhombuses, or with a trapezoid, a rhombus, and a triangle.

2. Remove the blocks and group them according to color. Then, count the number of each kind of block and record the information in the table provided on activity page 2.

3. Graph the results on activity page 2 by coloring one square in the graph for every two blocks.

Guided Learning

1. Which pattern block appears most on the graph?

2. Which pattern block appears least?
   Tan rhombus and square—both appear zero times.

Explore More!

Ask the students to create their own pictures with various pattern blocks. Then have them record the number of each block used in a table and bar graph (similar to the worksheet).

© Didax – www.didax.com

Name: _____

1. Cover the grid below using any of the pattern blocks to make an original design.

2. Remove the blocks and group them according to color.

3. Record the number of each kind you used in the spaces provided on the next page.

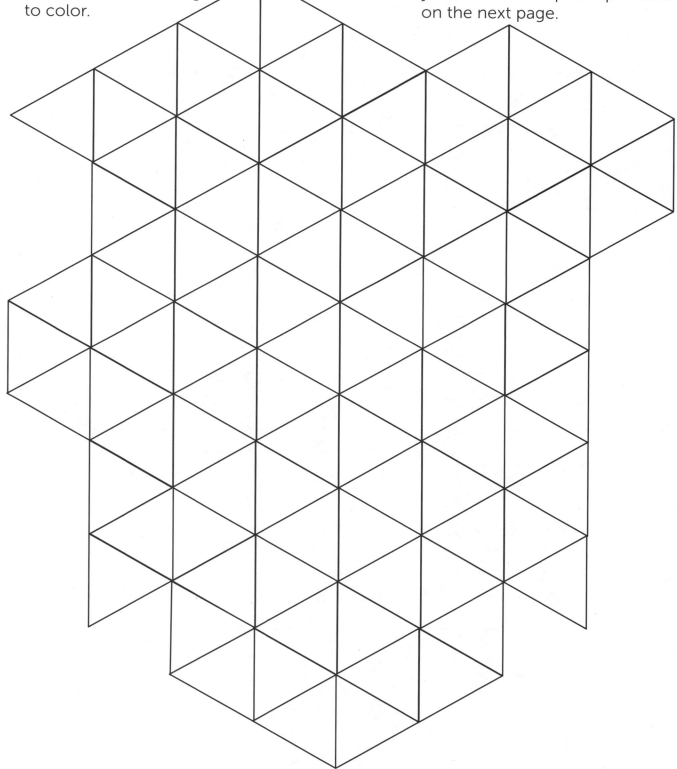

Name: _____

1. For my original design, I needed ... (fill in the blanks).

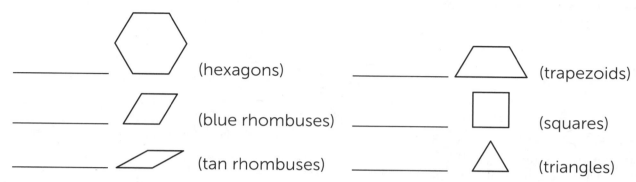

_____ ⬡ (hexagons)　　　　_____ ⏢ (trapezoids)

_____ ▱ (blue rhombuses)　　_____ ▢ (squares)

_____ ▱ (tan rhombuses)　　_____ △ (triangles)

2. For each number of pattern blocks you recorded in the table above, color the appropriate number of squares in the corresponding column of the graph below.

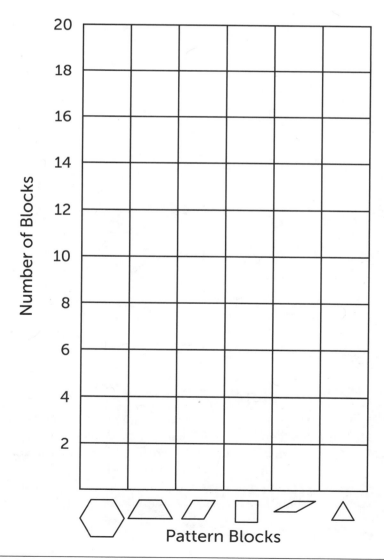

Focal Point

Statistics and Probability – Read bar graphs, analyze the data, and use them to answer questions.

Materials

- Pattern blocks

Instructions

Have the students read the bar graph and use it to fill in the table. Then, have them take the pattern blocks indicated in the table and make a design. They then copy their design on the back of the worksheet.

Guided Learning

1. How many of each block do you have?

2. Looking at the graph, are there more triangles or hexagons?

3. Which two pattern blocks, when combined, total the same number as the triangles? Explain.

4. How many pattern blocks did you use altogether? Explain how to find this number without counting the blocks individually.

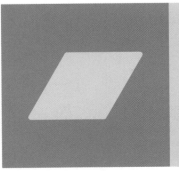

Explore More!

Have the students work in pairs. Students select a total of 40 blocks with no more than 10 of any one kind of block. One student in each pair makes a design and draws it on a sheet of paper. The other student makes a graph of the blocks. Separate the graphs and their designs and place them in different areas of the room. Then have the pairs of students try to match each graph to its correct design.

Design Your Way

Name: _____

1. Read the bar graph below. It shows the number of pattern blocks used in another original design.

2. Fill in the table below the graph, indicating how many of each pattern block was used in the design.

3. Take the pattern blocks indicated and make a design. Copy the design on the reverse side of this sheet.

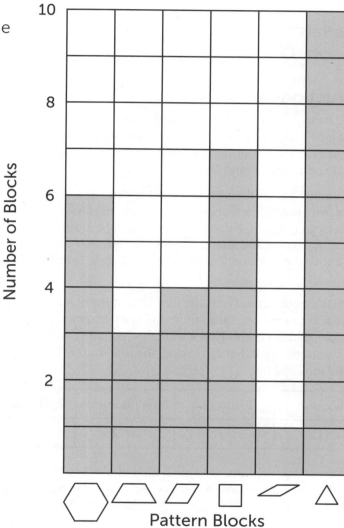

The following pattern blocks were used:

_____ (hexagons)   _____ (trapezoids)

_____ (blue rhombuses) _____ (squares)

_____ (tan rhombuses) _____ (triangles)

© Didax – www.didax.com   Advanced Pattern Block Book – **117**

Focal Point

Statistics and Probability – Collect and record data relating to an experiment. Use tallies to count data. Construct a frequency table to represent a collection of data. Display data in a bar graph.

Materials

• Pattern blocks

Instructions

Note: The experiment can be performed by one person taking all 4 handfuls (A–D) or by a pair of students, with Student #1 doing Experiments A and C and Student #2 doing Experiments B and D.

Experiment: Ask Student #1 to take a handful of pattern blocks from the bag or bucket without looking. Only 12 blocks are needed. Pattern blocks should be sorted according to color and shape and results recorded in the table above the diagonal line in the row labeled "Handful A."

Students should record only the first 12 pattern blocks they see. For example, if the student gets 2 hexagons, 1 trapezoid, 3 blue rhombuses, 4 triangles, 1 square, and 1 tan rhombus (a total of 12 blocks), the first line of the box will look like this:

Then, have the pairs of students do the same experiment three more times and compare the results, taking only 12 blocks each time from the bag (bucket) for Experiments B–D.

Guided Learning

1. Did you get the same results each time? Why or why not?

2. Did the results differ a lot? Why or why not?

Each of the fractions represents the number of a certain block selected out of a total of 12 blocks.

3. Why will the total always be 12/12?

4. What is another name for 12/12?

Hexagon	Trapezoid	Blue Rhombus	Triangle	Square	Tan Rhombus	Total
2/12	1/12	3/12	4/12	1/12	1/12	12/12

After recording the number of each kind of block in the table, the students return the blocks to the bag and mix them up. Mix the blocks by shaking the bag or bucket.

Explore More!

Have the students try this same experiment using fewer blocks, such as 6 or 8. If the original set of available blocks stays the same, why does the number of eack kind of pattern block change so often?

What would happen if you did NOT return the blocks after choosing and recording them? Would that change which blocks you actually chose? Why? Would the denominator of each fraction still be the same? Explain.

  © Didax – www.didax.com

Handfuls

Name: _____

1. Without looking, take a handful of at least 12 blocks from a bag of pattern blocks. Count out the first 12 blocks and return any additional blocks to the bag.

2. Sort the blocks according to color and record your results above the diagonal line in the row of the table labeled "Handful A."

3. Return the blocks to the bag, shake it to mix them up, and repeat the experiment 3 more times.

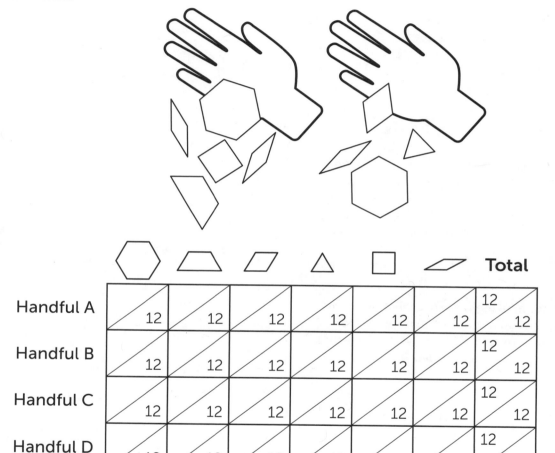

	⬡	⬠	▱	△	□	▱	Total
Handful A	12	12	12	12	12	12	12 / 12
Handful B	12	12	12	12	12	12	12 / 12
Handful C	12	12	12	12	12	12	12 / 12
Handful D	12	12	12	12	12	12	12 / 12

Write a mathematical sentence indicating the fractional parts and their sum for each experiment.

Experiment A: _____

Experiment B: _____

Experiment C: _____

Experiment D: _____

Focal Point

Statistics and Probability – Collect and record data relating to an experiment. Use blocks and exchanges to determine the "value" of a combination of blocks. Recognize that the value isn't changed when blocks are permuted.

Materials

- Pattern blocks
  - 3 green triangles
  - 3 blue rhombuses
  - 3 red trapezoids

Instructions

Put students in groups of 3 or 4. Students take 3 pattern blocks at a time out of the bag without looking. They record the combination of blocks—for example, GGG (3 green triangles), GGR (2 green triangles and 1 red trapezoid), and so on. They then replace the blocks in the bag and draw again. Have them repeat this experiment 12 times. The students can take turns drawing and recording.

Next, students determine the value of each drawing in triangles, exchanging the rhombus and trapezoid for triangles, if necessary, to determine the value. They then graph the results on the graph provided.

Guided Learning

1. Are combinations of GGR, GRG, and RGG considered to be different? Why or why not?

2. Which combinations appeared most often? Why?

3. Which combinations appeared least often? Why?

4. RBG and RGB each have a triangle value of 6. Which other combinations of pattern blocks have a triangle value of 6?

Explore More!

Combine the data from this experiment from all the groups and look at the distribution of blocks. Which combination appeared most often? Why do you think this is so?

© Didax – www.didax.com

Grab Bag

Name: _____

1. From a bag containing 3 green triangles, 3 blue rhombuses, and 3 red trapezoids, you will be drawing 3 blocks. All of the possible outcomes are listed for you below. Before doing the experiment, find the value in triangles for each possible outcome.

2. Now take 3 pattern blocks at a time out of the bag without looking. Record your results with a tally mark in the column labeled "Number of Times Drawn." Replace the blocks and repeat the experiment for a total of 12 trials.

3. Graph your findings on the graph.

Outcomes	Value in △s	Number of Times Drawn
3 △		
2 △, 1 ◇		
2 △, 1 ▱		
3 ◇		
2 ◇, 1 △		
2 ◇, 1 ▱		
3 ▱		
2 ▱, 1 △		
2 ▱, 1 ◇		
1 △, 1 ▱, 1 ◇		

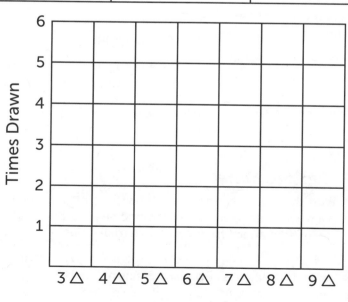

Focal Point

Statistics and Probability – Predict the outcome of an experiment. Conduct an experiment to test predictions. Compare the actual results to the predicted results. Describe the parts of the data and the data set as a whole to determine what the data show. Introduce the idea of likely outcomes.

Materials

- Pattern blocks
  - 6 orange squares
  - 1 blue rhombus
- Bag

Instructions

This is a "sampling experiment." Prepare a bag containing 7 pattern blocks (6 orange squares and 1 blue rhombus). Students do not know the exact contents. Shake the bag for the group.

Say: From a bucket of only orange squares and blue rhombuses, I put 7 blocks in a bag. These blocks can be only blue rhombuses or orange squares. What could be in the bag?
7 orange squares; 6 orange squares and 1 blue rhombus; 5 squares and 2 rhombuses; and so on.

Ask the students to record their guesses on the line labeled "My Prediction 1." Record all of the correct possibilities on the chalkboard and allow time for discussion.

Have a student shake the bag while you select one block and record it, making a tally on the chalkboard next to a drawing of either a square or rhombus. Return the block to the bag. Perform this selection process 5 times

in all. Then give the students an opportunity to make a new prediction about the blocks and record this as "My Prediction 2."

Ask: Did you change your prediction? Why?

Now students take additional samples, working in pairs. Let one student shake the bag while another student selects the block. Record the tally marks on the board while the students make tally marks on their papers under Sampling 3. After doing this 5 times, ask them to make another prediction ("My Prediction 3").

Ask: Did you change your prediction? Why?

Sampling 4: Have the students repeat the sampling experiment 10 more times, recording their tallies as before. Have them write their last prediction on the line for "My Prediction 4."

Ask: Did you change your prediction this time? Why?

At the board, record the number of students choosing each of the eight possibilities. After discussion, the secret of the bag is revealed.

Guided Learning

1. Did our class results match what was actually in the bag? Why or why not?

2. Which of the 8 possibilities would have a better chance for both the orange squares and blue rhombuses to appear the same number of times?

3. If all seven blocks were squares, what's the probability of picking a blue rhombus? Why?

4. If all seven blocks were blue rhombuses, what's the probability of picking a blue rhombus? Why?

Explore More!

Was the orange square or the blue rhombus selected more often? Why were we more likely to pick the orange square? Would you make a better prediction after 5 trials or after 25 trials? Why?

Tell the students they need many trials to get a good estimate. Have them imagine their own "secret bag of blocks" and describe it in their math journal. Have them explain which block is more likely to be picked.

© Didax – www.didax.com

Sampling

From a bucket containing only orange squares and blue rhombuses, 7 blocks are put in a bag.

On the line labeled "My Prediction 1," record how many of each kind of block you think are in the bag. While the experiment is being conducted, tally which block appears each time and change your prediction according to the new information.

My Prediction 1   □ _____   ◇ _____

My Prediction 2   □ _____   ◇ _____

Sampling 3

□ _____

Tally

◇ _____

Tally

My Prediction 3   □ _____   ◇ _____

Sampling 4

□ _____

Tally

◇ _____

Tally

My Prediction 4   □ _____   ◇ _____

Focal Point

Statistics and Probability – Predict the outcome of an experiment. Conduct an experiment to test predictions. Compare actual results to predicted results. Describe parts of the data and the data set as a whole to determine what the data show. Introduce the idea of likely outcomes.

Materials

- Pattern blocks
  - orange squares
  - blue rhombuses
- A bag for each pair of students

Instructions

Place 10 blocks in a bag, chosen from orange squares and blue rhombuses only. Make up enough bags for every pair of students in the class. Give one copy of the worksheet to each pair of students. Designate one student as Student A and the other as Student B

Say: The bags contain only orange squares and blue rhombuses. Each bag has only 10 blocks. Guess how many of each kind of block are in your bag.

Tell the students to record their guess on the worksheet under #1, First Prediction. Now they should do the experiments.

Experiment 1: Repeat 10 times. Students quickly remove only 1 block each time without feeling the other blocks. They tally the results and return the block to the bag. When they have finished, ask them to record a prediction based on the results under #2, Second Prediction.

Ask: Did your prediction change? Why?

Experiment 2: Repeat the procedure used in Experiment 1 20 more times. Students tally the results and record a revised prediction under #3, Third Prediction.

After a class discussion, have the students make a final prediction under #4. Then have them take the blocks out of the bag and see if their prediction was correct.

Guided Learning

1. Was your initial prediction what was actually in the bag? Why or why not?

2. Was your final prediction closer to what was actually in the bag? Why or why not?

3. What prediction has a probability of "0" (impossible)?

4. Which arrangement would give the blue rhombus and the orange square an equal chance of being selected? Why?

5. Which arrangements would give an orange square a more likely chance of being selected? Why?

6. Which arrangements would give a blue rhombus a more likely chance of being selected? Why?

Explore More!

In their math journal, have the students design an experiment for 15 blocks from a bag of blue rhombuses and trapezoids. Have them explain which arrangements would give each block the best chance of being selected. Why?

Discuss how to change the contents of a bag so that the selection of an orange square would be certain; so that the selection of an orange square would be impossible; and so that the selection of an orange square would be just as likely as the selection of a blue rhombus.

© Didax – www.didax.com

Making Predictions

Name: _____

An Activity for 2 Students

1. The 10 pattern blocks in the bag can only be squares or blue rhombuses. Make a first prediction about how many of each are in the bag and record your guess in the space provided for Student A or B.

2. Remove a block, record the result, return the block, and shake the bag. Do this 10 times. Revise your prediction based on the results and record it in the spaces next to "Second Prediction."

3. Then do the same experiment 20 more times (Experiment 2). Based on the results, revise your description again and record it in the spaces next to "Third Prediction."

4. After a class discussion, write your "final prediction" in the space provided.

1. First Prediction   Student A   ☐ _____   ◇ _____

Student B   ☐ _____   ◇ _____

Experiment 1   ☐   ◇

2. Second Prediction   Student A   ☐ _____   ◇ _____

Student B   ☐ _____   ◇ _____

Experiment 2   ☐   ◇

3. Third Prediction   Student A   ☐ _____   ◇ _____

Student B   ☐ _____   ◇ _____

4. We think our bag contains _____

5. We were correct!   or

We should have guessed   ☐ _____   ◇ _____

Focal Point

Statistics and Probability – Understand and apply concepts of probability.

Materials

- Pattern blocks
  - 4 squares
  - 1 blue rhombus
  - 3 red trapezoids
  - 2 hexagons

Instructions

Have the students look at the table on the worksheet. Tell them that for the first rule, labeled "hexagon," there are only 2 hexagons in the group of pattern blocks.

Say: In row 1, why are the square, rhombus, and trapezoid marked with an X in the "Belong" column? Why does the hexagon have a "2" in it?

In the "Do Not Belong" column, the hexagon has been eliminated, and the number of squares (4), rhombuses (1), and trapezoids (3) are shown.

Ask: What do the numbers 4, 1, and 3 indicate in the column marked "Do Not Belong"? How many blocks belong in the family? *2*

How many blocks do NOT belong? *8—those that are NOT hexagons. The number "8" is in the "Total – Do Not Belong" column.*

Tell students that for each row of the table, they should separate the blocks into two groups: those that belong and those that do not belong. Each row poses a rule, and the students should record their answers according to the rule. Some of the subsets will be empty.

Guided Learning

Note: In matters of probability, "or" is inclusive—that is, the group "red blocks or blue blocks" includes all the red blocks and also all the blue blocks. So, you may count both red blocks AND blue blocks as part of the subset.

1. What do we mean by the rule "orange or hexagon"?

2. What do we mean by the rule "yellow or polygon"?

3. What do we mean by the rule "quadrilaterals and parallelograms"?

4. What do we mean by the rule "octagons and yellow"?

5. Why is the total of the "Belong" and "Do Not Belong" columns always 10?

6. How many members are there for the rule (subset) of red and parallelogram? Explain.

Explore More!

Have the students take any 12 pattern blocks, make four new rules, and decide which blocks belong and which blocks do not belong according to each rule. Remind them that the total (in the family) must equal 12. Have them include one rule with "and" and one rule with "or." Note: This activity introduces the concept of complement.

© Didax – www.didax.com

All in the Family

Name: _____

1. Look at the first rule, "hexagon." Only 2 hexagons are members of that "family" of pattern blocks. Therefore, 2 blocks of the set "rule" "belong" to that family and 8 blocks "do not belong."

2. Indicate which blocks belong or do not belong according to their set "rule" in each row.

3. Complete the columns labeled "Total."

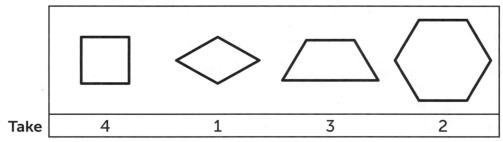

Rule	Belong	Do Not Belong	Total Belong	Total Do Not Belong
hexagon			2	8
red				
orange or green				
trapezoid				
blue or square				
red or blue				
quadrilateral and a parallelogram				
yellow or a polygon				
orange or a hexagon				
an octagon and yellow				

© Didax – www.didax.com

Focal Point

Statistics and Probability – Understand and apply concepts of probability. Use fractions/ratios to record experimental results.

Materials

• Pattern blocks

Instructions

Tell the students that each target on the worksheet is made of 3 different pattern blocks. They are to determine the probability that the smallest block will be hit if they throw a ball at the target randomly. What is the probability that the largest block will be hit?

Have the students use their pattern blocks to find which three blocks make up each target and then sketch them on the worksheet.

Ask: How many triangles cover the entire target? How many triangles cover the smallest block?

The probability of hitting the smallest block is the fraction composed of the number of triangles in the smallest block divided by the number of triangles in the entire target.

Ask: How would you find the probability of hitting the largest block?

Guided Learning

1. What is the triangle value of Target A? Target B? Target C?

2. What is the triangle value of the smallest pattern block in Target A? Target B? Target C?

The probability of hitting the smallest pattern block is expressed as P(S).

P(S) = triangle value of the smallest pattern block

triangle value of the total target

3. What is the probability of hitting the smallest pattern block in Target A? Target B? Target C?

4. What is the triangle value of the largest pattern block in Target A? Target B? Target C?

The probability of hitting the largest pattern block is expressed as P(L).

P(L) = triangle value of the largest pattern block

triangle value of the total target

5. What is the probability of hitting the largest pattern block in Target A? Target B? Target C?

Explore More!

Have the students draw two more targets, one using 2 blocks and one using 3 blocks. They may use only triangles, blue rhombuses, trapezoids, or hexagons. Have them determine P(S) and P(L) for each.

© Didax – www.didax.com

Name: _____

Each target below (A, B, and C) is made of three different pattern blocks. Find the probability that the smallest block would be hit if you threw a ball at the target randomly. What is the probability that the largest block in the target would be hit?

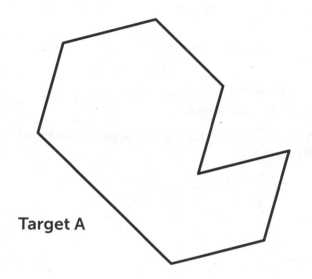

Target A

$$P(S) = \frac{\triangle \text{ covering smallest block} = 1}{\triangle \text{ covering total target} = 9}$$

$P(L) = $ _____

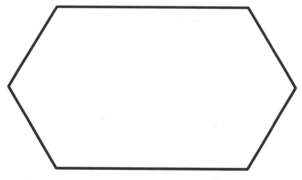

Target B

$P(S) = $ _____

$P(L) = $ _____

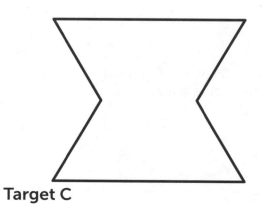

Target C

$P(S) = $ _____

$P(L) = $ _____

Focal Point

Statistics and Probability – Understand and apply concepts of probability. Use fractions/ratios to record experimental results.

Materials

• Pattern blocks

Instructions

Have the students use their pattern blocks to find which four pieces make up each target. Each of these targets contains four pattern blocks, and some blocks may be identical.

Find at least two solutions for each target. If two or more blocks are the smallest (or largest) blocks in the target, students should give the combined triangle value of these blocks as the answer.

Guided Learning

1. What is the triangle value of the entire target?

2. What is the triangle value of the smallest pattern block(s) in the target?

The probability of hitting the smallest pattern block is expressed as P(S).

$$P(S) = \frac{\text{triangle value of the smallest pattern block(s)}}{\text{triangle value of the total target}}$$

3. What is the triangle value of the largest pattern block(s) in the target?

The probability of hitting the largest pattern block is expressed as P(L).

$$P(L) = \frac{\text{triangle value of the largest pattern block(s)}}{\text{triangle value of the total target}}$$

Explore More!

Have the students take turns writing and solving probability problems that are similar to the following: Make a 4-piece target so that P(S) = 2/10 and P(L) = 6/10.

© Didax – www.didax.com

Hitting the Bulls-Eye

Name: _____

1. Take 4 pattern blocks to cover targets A, B, and C. Some of the blocks in each target may be identical.

2. Find the probability of hitting the largest pattern blocks and the smallest pattern blocks in each target.

3. Cover each target in two different ways.

Target A

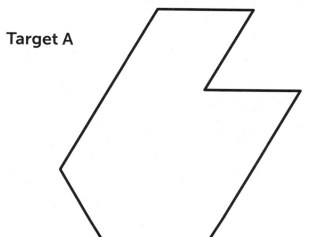

Solution 1   Solution 2

P(S) = _____   P(S) = _____

P(L) = _____   P(L) = _____

Target B

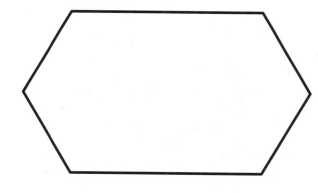

Solution 1   Solution 2

P(S) = _____   P(S) = _____

P(L) = _____   P(L) = _____

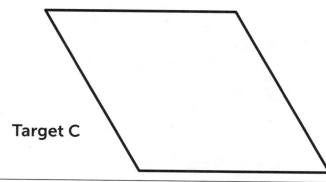

Solution 1   Solution 2

P(S) = _____   P(S) = _____

Target C

P(L) = _____   P(L) = _____

Focal Point

Statistics and Probability – Develop and practice collecting and recording data in an organized way to determine all the possible outcomes. Formulate conclusions and make predictions from experiments.

Materials

- Pattern blocks
- 4 bags

Instructions/Guided Learning

Prepare 4 bags ahead of time, as follows:

Bag A: 4 of each block except hexagons; 20 blocks total

Bag B: 10 blue rhombuses and 10 trapezoids

Bag C: 15 squares and 5 tan rhombuses

Bag D: 1 hexagon and 19 triangles

Each group of students will investigate all 4 bags, so you may wish to prepare multiple sets or do the experiment in front of the class with students using the resulting data.

Students work in small groups (3 or 4 students, preferably) and perform experiments to determine what each bag contains and in what proportions (fractions). Tell them there are 20 blocks in each bag.

Students must devise a step-by-step procedure to perform the probability experiment without looking inside the bag. Students describe their experiments in their math journals.

The experiment for each bag should be performed a minimum of five times by each member of the group. The results of each experiment are compiled, graphed, and used to make predictions. Record all results before revealing the contents of each bag.

A whole-class discussion at the end of this lesson comparing step-by-step procedures, organization, results, and predictions is helpful in furthering student learning. The experiments may take more than one class period.

Explore More!

Given bags B, C, and D, have the students write the probability (P) of choosing each type of block if they selected one randomly from the given bag. For example, if they are selecting from Bag B, they find P(blue rhombus) and P(trapezoid).

Name: _____

Number of Blocks (y-axis: 2, 4, 6, 8, 10, 12, 14, 16, 18, 20)

Pattern Blocks

Number of Blocks (y-axis: 2, 4, 6, 8, 10, 12, 14, 16, 18, 20)

Pattern Blocks

Number of Blocks (y-axis: 2, 4, 6, 8, 10, 12, 14, 16, 18, 20)

Pattern Blocks

Number of Blocks (y-axis: 2, 4, 6, 8, 10, 12, 14, 16, 18, 20)

Pattern Blocks

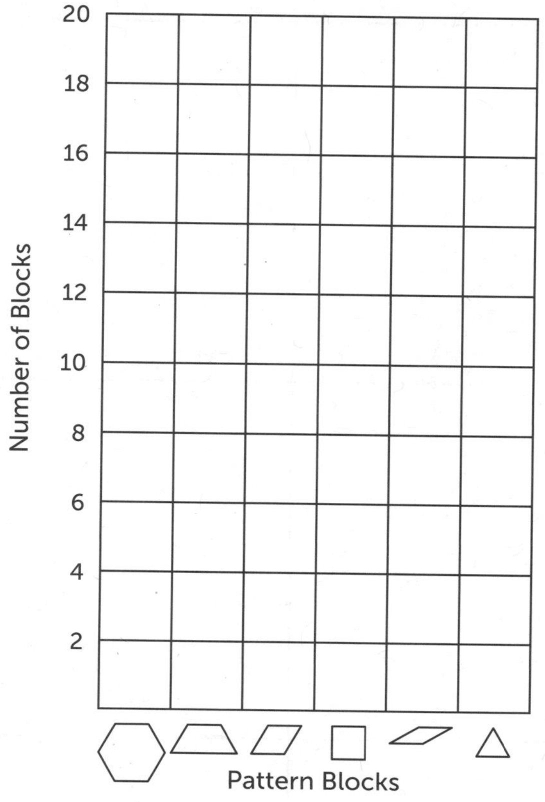

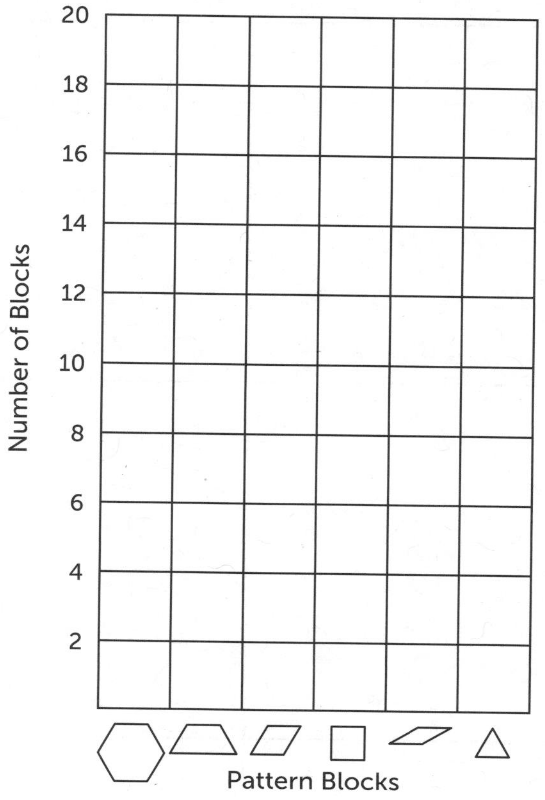

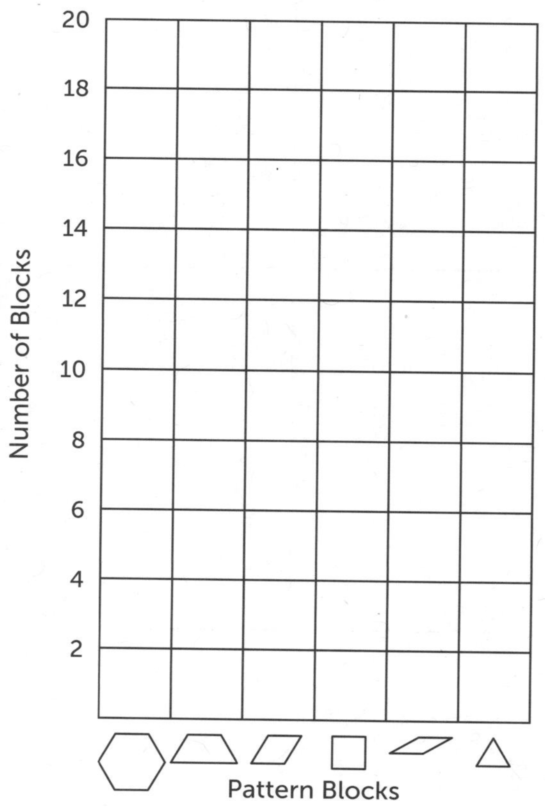

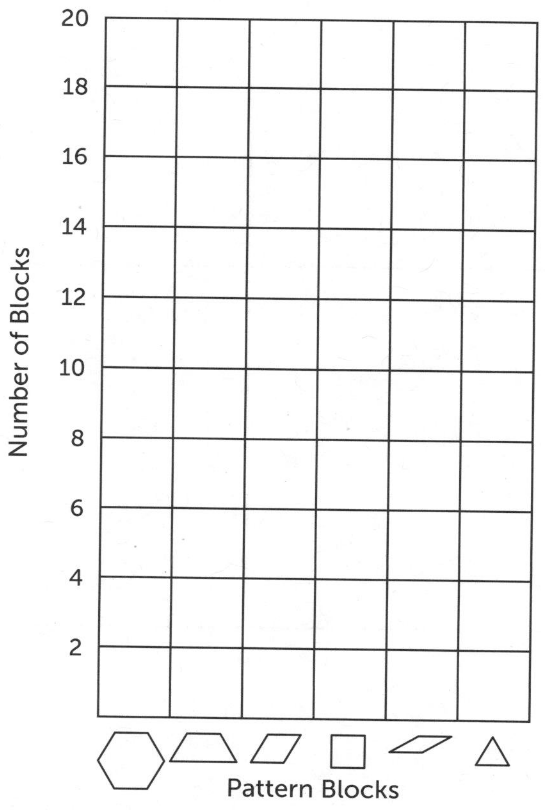

<table>
<tr><td></td><td></td><td></td><td></td></tr>
<tr><td></td><td></td><td></td><td></td></tr>
<tr><td></td><td></td><td></td><td></td></tr>
<tr><td></td><td></td><td></td><td></td></tr>
</table>

© Didax – www.didax.com

© Didax – www.didax.com

© Didax – www.didax.com